Leslie

You Fall Off,
You Get Back On

You Fall Off, You Get Back On

11-13-14

*Leslie,
Miss seeing you
at domes.
Hope you enjoy
this
love
Mary Stobie*

Mary Stobie

Liberator Press
Denver, Colorado

You Fall Off, You Get Back On: A Patchwork Memoir
by Mary Stobie

Published in the United States by Liberator Press, Denver, Colorado

All columns attributed to the Colorado Community Media newspapers originally appeared in one or more of the following publications: *The Golden Transcript, The Wheat Ridge Transcript, Lakewood Sentinel* and *Arvada Press.* These columns are reprinted courtesy of Colorado Community Media.

Permission granted by the *Chicago Tribune* to reprint the columns "Always the Hero" and "Becoming a Soccer Mom." "Sentimental" and "Afghanistan Hits Home" are reprinted courtesy of *The Denver Post.* Permission granted by *Canyon Courier* to reprint "Beatletoast," "Family Is Where the Love Is," "Dare to Be Disorganized," "On Entering the Mysterious World of … Science," "Tales from Lake McConaughy," "Day on the Prairie," "Defining Roles for Women," "It's Christmas Time," "Why Shouldn't Older Women have Babies?" "The Wild West is Still Alive in Yellowstone," and "Climbing Fools."

Some of the columns have been edited for this book.

ISBN: 978-0-692-30113-5
ISBN, Library Edition: 978-1-5028-4700-3

Cover and interior design by Nick Zelinger, NZ Graphics.com

Front cover photo of Mary McFerren Stobie, age four, by Betty McFerren, 1951
Back cover author photo by Lily Ribeiro, 2014

For information about special discounts for bulk purchases, contact Mary Stobie at info@MaryStobie.com.

For more information about the author, visit www.MaryStobie.com.

First Edition
Printed in the United States of America

For Noah and Bianca

What is life? It is the flash of a firefly in the night. It is the breath of a buffalo in the wintertime. It is the little shadow which runs across the grass and loses itself in the sunset.
—Crowfoot, Blackfoot warrior and orator

Table of Contents

Author's Note

I've structured this book to follow the flow of my life. Much of this work comprises reprinted columns, several of which encompass three decades, such as those about my mom and dad. When in doubt, I've placed those pieces where they just feel right.

Because many of these essays appeared originally as newspaper columns, and others I wrote recently about my early life, you'll see stylistic variety. I hope this hodgepodge of paper scraps and old photos bonds together into one life's colorful fabric—my patchwork memoir.

Mary Stobie

You Fall Off, You Get Back On

Part One

Learning the Ropes
in My Family Corral

When we show our respect for other living things,
they respond with respect for us.
—Arapaho proverb

1

Learning to Ride

When I was three, my cowgirl mother taught me how to ride a horse. She began our lessons by helping me clamber up on the bare back of our bay mare, Queenie. Queenie's soft, round body welcomed me. Grasping the coarse hair of her black mane, I laid my cheek down against her brown furry neck. Everything felt so familiar, perhaps because while pregnant with me, my mother went riding. Even before I was born I felt the rhythm of a galloping horse.

For my first real riding lesson, Mom saddled up Queenie, lifted me aboard, and adjusted the stirrups up high for my legs. At first I clung to the horn, but I soon learned how to sit in the saddle with my boots secure in the stirrups. "Keep your heels down, Mary," Mom said. "The reins go in your left hand so you can open a gate or rope a calf with your right hand."

I listened. I felt at home in the saddle on Queenie. Before long we moved around the ring at a walk, trot, and gallop.

As I got older I learned to groom Queenie. The taller I grew, the higher I could brush her on her shoulders and rump. Each day before riding, my mother lifted Queenie's hooves so I could gently pry out the rocks and mud with a blunt screwdriver.

With an open palm, I gave Queenie crisp carrots and red apples. She nuzzled them gently off my hand and crunched them greedily. We put our nostrils close together and inhaled each other's breath, creating friendship beyond words.

These early experiences with Queenie gave me self-confidence and comfort around horses, a godsend. My mother may have started me riding early because I was born with flat feet and bowlegs. The doctor prescribed metal braces for me to wear on my legs after school and at night. My friend Martha McKenna watched my mother put on the braces.

"Does that hurt?" she asked.

"The metal is cold," I said.

For school I wore clunky shoes with laces tied up to my ankles, never cute flats with straps like the other girls. Cowboy boots felt the most comfortable of any footwear. Every afternoon after school when I put them on, in my mind I became a real cowgirl. Finally I kicked off the braces forever. Hurrah!

⁓

My leg braces are off. My parents, my older brother, Bill, and I take a pack trip in the high Sierra Mountains of California. We start at Courtright Reservoir and ride up the steep trails in exposed granite areas toward "Hell for Sure Pass."

We ride separately on our assigned horses heading for our destination, Hell for Sure Lake, following our packer who guides us. After four hours in the saddle I'm hot and tired. I spot the lake and inhale the scent of the pine trees. The air is clean and crisp. Dragonflies float nearby and I hear insects buzzing.

The packer-guide unsaddles the horses and takes them to graze.

The lake beckons to my fisherman father, and the rest of us join him, throwing in our lines, and between us we catch enough trout for dinner. With a razor-sharp knife, my father slits the white trout bellies and removes the guts. My mother rinses the trout, rolls them in cornmeal, and lays them in a cast iron frying pan over a green Coleman camping stove. After twenty minutes of cooking the trout and sliced potatoes in the fresh mountain air, we eat. Our dinner tastes better than at home.

Our descent from the lake a few days later is faster and more difficult than the climb; I notice now that the trail disappears in many spots. My horse's hooves clatter on the slabs of granite—she slip-slides, choosing her own path down. A horsefly lands on her shoulder and I slap it dead. My legs are sore; a dark cloud covers the sun.

As we ride toward the rendezvous point with the horse trailers, we hear a rumbling. Louder and louder, until the noise blasts our ears. A colossal dump truck barrels past us full speed ahead. My horse spooks and bolts in a panic, racing away from the rest of the group, faster and faster. Terrified, sore, and trembling, I cling to the saddle horn and pull back on the reins with all my might. "Whoa, stop!" I holler. But I am no match for the mare's strength. She bucks and loosens the grip of my legs and sends me sailing through the air. My body crashes down onto the hard gravel road. Ouch, double ouch, I hurt all over—I have the wind knocked out of me, with bleeding elbows, torn jeans, and rocks and dirt in my hair. When I catch my breath, I cry and wail, "Help, help! I need help."

Moments later my family rides up next to me on their horses. After dismounting and checking me over to make sure I'm not seriously injured, my mother buzzes louder than a wasp. She gallops off on her horse, chasing the truck, racing full speed. I dust myself off and my father puts Band-Aids on my elbows.

When Mom returns, she says, "The truck driver pulled over and I said, 'Mister, I'll give you a piece of my mind. Don't you know enough to slow down when you pass horses? You spooked my daughter's horse, which caused a nasty fall. She could have been killed!' The truck driver said to me, 'Woman, I'll give you a piece of my mind back. I work for the Bechtel Corporation. We have a dam to build!' And that sucker drove off leaving me spitting out dust."

"What a toad," I said.

My brother, Bill, catches my horse and leads her back to me.

As they say in the horse world, "You fall off, you get back on."

And that's what I do.

San Mateo, California, 1950–1952

My first riding lesson on Queenie, 1950

2

Beware of Bad Horses

They say you have to kiss a lot of frogs to meet a good man.
The same is true with horses: You may have to ride many
dangerous ones before you find a safe steed.

After we moved to Golden, Colorado, so my father could start a food brokerage business and my mother could have a horse corral on our property, the first pony my parents bought was a fat little rascal, Poncho. He threw me and dragged me back to the barn with my boot caught in the stirrup. A good horse would stand still if his rider was hung up, until the rider could right herself, but not Poncho. He dragged me like I was a sack of potatoes, banging my head along the ground. I lost a hunk of hair snagged in a Canadian thistle bush. After freeing my foot and boot back at the stable, I thanked God I was still alive. My parents sold Poncho—gone, gone, gone.

One day I rode a tall new mare, Creole, to the top of the mesa on South Table Mountain behind our house. The trails were full of spiny yuccas and loose rocks. On the way home the bratty horse raced down the hill toward the barn with the bit clenched in her teeth so I couldn't stop her no matter how hard I pulled. My face flushed as terror shot through me. "Whoa, stop, you crazy horse!"

She tossed me off. Crash-boom.

"Darn horse!" I yelled. "I hope my parents sell you to the rodeo to be a bronco. When I get older I'll ride you to win a buckle for staying on!"

In spite of bad experiences with Poncho and Creole, I didn't give up. I fell off, I got on again. With my own money I saved, I bought Smoky, a small black horse. He was a gem with a sweet disposition. I made friends with neighborhood girls and boys who all rode horses: Claudia Brundage, Judy Haberl, Pam Pearson, Manet Oshier, Tia Tyler. Doug Buzard and Bobby Brendan, who had horses, also joined us on rides. We rode around the gravel roads in the Applewood Mesa area of Golden, and raced our horses on the dirt airstrip on Bobby's parents' place. Gone now, of course, long replaced with suburban homes.

One day a cowboy parked in front of my family's corral with a horse trailer. My mother and I went out to see what was up. The man unloaded a lovely buckskin mare and said, "She's for sale, only $100." My mother's eyes lit up.

She couldn't resist a bargain and luck was with us—Twinkle was a real find. She was high spirited, had a great willingness, and always tried to please us. Twinkle was worth the wait. I entered horse shows and rodeos with Twinkle. We did well, winning trophies and ribbons in barrel racing, pole bending, and goat tying. Giving it her best in every event, Twinkle became the most loved horse my family ever owned.

Golden, Colorado, 1956

Sack race on Twinkle, 1959

3

A Wild Ride

As a teenager, I competed in Little Britches Rodeos, which had the slogan "Where Legends Begin." Little Britches Rodeos emphasized good sportsmanship. My mother and father hauled me and my buckskin mare, Twinkle, to rodeos all over the state of Colorado. The youth rodeos formed a traveling community for contestants, and many lasting friendships formed. As a youth competitor, my best events were barrel racing, goat tying, pole bending, and horse racing.

M y best friend at Little Britches Rodeos is Jon Vierk, a cute cowboy with striking blue eyes. He typically wears a red vest and a white cowboy hat. One day he says, "Mary, the bucking events are the most exciting. Have you thought of entering Girls Steer Riding?"

"Sounds scary," I say, but I want to impress Jon, who is a top bull rider. "I'll try it." Without knowing how difficult it will be, I sign up for girls steer riding at the Little Britches Rodeo at Arapahoe County Fairgrounds in Littleton.

I imagine I'll hold the rigging, squeeze the steer's sides with my legs—and the animal will run in a straight line. I've ridden horses since I was three. A steer should be no problem.

Or so I think.

Even though I appear like a brave cowgirl wearing a flowered western shirt, jeans, and boots, I feel petrified as I approached the bucking chutes—it isn't the horses that spook me, it's the cowboys watching me.

I am about to risk my neck riding a hairy monster.

My heart calls out, "Whoa! Halt! Stop, no, no, no!"

But I reassure myself, Taking risks is what makes life worth living. And I do it anyway.

Hoping to win a prize, I climb onto my assigned bucking chute. Jon waits, ready to assist me with the rigging. I gape at the steer—a huge Scottish Highlander with a shaggy red coat. His horns are so long he could play in an orchestra. I feel dizzy for a moment as I stare at him.

This creature knows he's Scottish, and like Braveheart he prepares for battle, snorting like a demon.

"Calm down before you ride," Jon says to me. "Take a deep breath."

I suck the pungent air into my lungs and gasp.

After Jon helps me get seated on the steer, I grip the handhold of the rigging. The steer shifts his body from side to side.

On his back, I am the enemy.

I say, "Hoot Mon, you think you can make light work of this rookie. But I'm Scottish, too, so this ride will be one Scot on top of another. Just don't go too crazy."

The announcer says, "The cowgirl in chute number four is Mary McFerren from Golden, Colorado. She's riding a long-haired hippie steer named Big Red. It's the first ride for this young lady, so cheer her on."

The crowd roars.

The gate clanks open.

The Scottish monster's first jump out of the chute shows off his power. As he twists sideways, I feel unbelievable tugs on my shoulder and elbow joints. My hand clutches the rigging for dear life. Determination fires up in me, and hanging on with every twist and turn, my body is jarred and wrenched like a rag doll.

My arms and neck hurt, my hat flies off, and it feels like my head is still in it!

"Come on, Mary, you can do it!" Jon hollers.

Three seconds feels like three hundred years.

Big Red does the Twist, Stomp, Jerk, Watusi, and Bugaloo for five, six, seven, eight seconds. When the bell buzzes, I do a half gainer into the arena dirt.

Phtooie!

I spring to my feet and strut back to the chutes. The crowd claps wildly.

"That's what you call determination," the announcer says over the loudspeaker. "This cowgirl earns a second-place buckle. Congratulations, Mary McFerren."

Wow. For my ride I am awarded a cool buckle decorated with a gold figure of a girl riding a steer. Waving it proudly, I show it to Jon and my parents.

"Mary, that was a sensational ride," my mother says.

Overcoming my fear and riding that red hairy steer makes me feel victorious. My mother says that steer riding builds my self-confidence.

Jon says after my steer ride, "Ain't this living?"

"Yes, this is living!"

Arapahoe County Fairgrounds, Littleton, Colorado, 1960

Barrel Race on Twinkle, 1960

4

Comet Becomes Seabiscuit in His Mind

At thirteen, due to my flat feet, I don't qualify for junior high track. My father, wanting me to excel at a sport, locates a registered quarter horse, Comet, a shiny bay gelding with white socks. I test ride him and get a big smile on my face. We decide to buy him.

Whoa, this is serious horseflesh! Now I feel pressure to win competitions.

I ride Comet around South Table Mountain behind our house. He doesn't spook at rabbits, dogs, or blowing plastic bags—too much effort in his book, I believe. Watching him with his slow walk and eyes half open, my friend Claudia says, "Your father bought you a lazy horse."

But Comet, like Dr. Jekyll and Mr. Hyde, has two personalities. I put him next to Claudia's horse, Pepper, to run a race up McIntyre Street. Every dormant cell in his body wakes up as if he'd had a dozen cups of espresso coffee. Sensing direct competition, that poky walk converts into fast prancing steps. He tugs on the reins ready to go. We race and Comet wins.

That summer I enter him in the Little Britches National Finals at Arapahoe County Fairgrounds in Littleton.

To get ready for the "Jr. Girls Pony Race" ("pony race" my eye— we all rode full-size horses), I brush Comet and saddle him. The silver Conchos on my saddle reflect sunlight with a high sheen.

The track smells of freshly plowed dirt and horses. From the crowd in the grandstands, the scent of popcorn wafts down.

The competition invigorates me. I squeeze Comet with my thighs and grip the reins. "Get ready to win this race, Comet," I say. "Every second counts." Comet winds himself up like a slingshot.

The race official calls out to the eight contestants. "Line up, line up." The other girls line up their horses—palominos, buckskins, and blacks—horses that look like they just came off the professional race-track.

I'm too nervous to stand still, so I circle Comet behind the chalk starting line. He smells the race, I can tell. We are both hyped up, and Comet feels my energy.

He lifts his front legs off the ground, just back of the starting line.

The official points his gun into the air, crack-boom.

My horse bolts forward like a shooting star, throwing me backwards. I grab the saddle horn and clutch the reins. The balls of my feet press into my boots against the stirrups full force. I lean forward, squeezing my thighs tighter against Comet's sides. The thunder of hooves sounds like a giant hailstorm.

My adrenaline pumps to the highest level as we race full-tilt-boogie down the dirt track. Mary Jane Blakeslee, a top competitor from Missoula, Montana, races next to me, her horse nosing ever closer to our right side. I urge Comet, "Come on, Comet, go! Go!" I swear Comet becomes Seabiscuit in his mind, a hot-blooded racehorse. We are both on fire, full of life at full throttle.

We pound across the finish line. The crowd roars. I hear the announcer's voice, "Mary McFerren from Golden, Colorado, riding Comet, first place. National champion pony racer." I howl with joy, and after we circle back and slow down I dismount and hug Comet's neck. "You did it! You did it!"

If I were a gymnast I would have done cartwheels and handsprings down the track in front of the grandstand. I'm so happy to think I'd won a championship at the Little Britches National Finals! Glowing, I receive the trophy and hold it proudly.

"Great riding, Mary," says my mother dressed in jeans and boots. "I didn't know how much fire Comet had in him."

Feeling ebullient and elated, I think: *So what if I am the slowest foot racer in junior high? I am the fastest girl on a track with Comet.*

Atop Comet, my physical skills improved. I continued to compete, and sometimes win, on Comet throughout my teens. I loved every minute. I could have conned people to race against me on Comet, as he looked so slow. But when I was ready to race, and Comet was ready to race, our readiness met opportunity and we excelled.

The world opened up for me when I got it right. But I had to get it right: Choose the right horse, practice with him and form a bond, and then choose the right event. I was good at riding steers and running the barrel race, but Comet was good at straight-out running. He didn't excel in barrel racing. He didn't see the point.

"Why run around those barrels?" he seemed to ask. But against another horse, he caught on. We were both at our best at those moments, good at the same thing, enjoying, loving, and treasuring the race.

Like Comet, I had to find what I was good at and ignore the rest. I was built inside and out to become one with a horse.

Comet was born to run. And I was born to ride.

Golden, Colorado, 1960

Comet the lazy horse wins high-point trophy, 1963.

5

Stealing a Barrel Horse

In 1963, when I was sixteen, Comet developed hoof problems. I couldn't run him for a year. He stayed on in our corral, as I cared for him and prayed he'd heal. "You'll make it, buddy," I told him. In April that year I searched for an additional horse, one that would run the cloverleaf barrel race—a timed event racing around three barrels in the rodeo arena.

In Fort Collins, north of Denver, a quarter horse auction is to be held in the evening. Hours before the auction, I arrive with my truck and horse trailer and enter the auction barn. The smell of alfalfa hay fills my nostrils. Various quarter horses wait in their stalls. A handsome brown gelding with excellent confirmation—a powerful rear end, solid chest, and a beautiful head with a gentle gaze—hangs his head over the stall door. He nickers at me.

I stroke his soft muzzle. The tall owner with a matching shirt and jeans tips his straw hat at me and smiles. "Hello, ma'am."

"Howdy, sir," I say. "I'll bet he can run."

The owner says, "Understatement, ma'am. Would you like to try him?"

I nod and the owner saddles up the horse named Yeager Ichi Bon. Then he confesses to me what might be considered a deal-breaker.

"You can't put a bit in his mouth. He has a scar and has to be ridden with a hackamore."

When I open and inspect Yeager's mouth, I gasp. A deep crevice runs across his long pink tongue in the spot a bit would fit. I shudder. A heavy-handed rider must have used a cruel bit to cause such an injury to this handsome horse.

The hackamore with the piece that goes over his nose uses pressure to stop him. I mount Yeager and walk him out of the barn. Quickly I know that in spite of this horse's injured tongue, I will buy him. He feels great and has a spirited walk. The owner says, "I'll get at least $2,000 for him in the auction."

Taken aback, I hesitate because I don't have that much money. After I ride him around the auction arena, I feel convinced he is the horse for me.

That night the auction begins with the auctioneer rapping over the microphone, hyping up the buyers. Riders move into the arena one at a time, on horses to be offered to the highest bidder. "Going once, going twice, sold," the auctioneer says over the loudspeaker. The pungent smell of dust from the arena fills my nostrils. Sitting in the grandstand full of buyers, I am ready to bid on Yeager.

With his owner mounted on him, Yeager waits outside the arena. "Next horse, Yeager Ichi Bon from Kansas." Yeager balks at the gate. The owner kicks Yeager's sides with spurs, urging him on, but a mysterious luck is with me—Yeager won't enter the arena.

Obviously he has had some bad experiences with people. Maybe his tongue has been cut in an arena, a hurtful experience with his mouth, something he won't ever forget. Like when I was a child and the dentist filled the cavity in my tooth without Novocain. Ouch!

Yeager repeatedly refuses to enter the arena. The auctioneer eliminates him from the sale. The owner rides him dejectedly back into the barn, with me following.

"I'm sorry about your bad luck," I say. "You probably don't want to haul him all the way back to Kansas."

"You got that right, ma'am."

"I'll give you $500 for him."

He dismounts and turns toward me. "Sold!"

Full of gladness, I write a check and hand it to the owner. He signs over Yeager's registration papers to me. I pet Yeager and say, "You're mine now."

Delighted to have such a fabulous horse for such a low price, I pinch myself to make sure I'm not dreaming.

After loading Yeager in my horse trailer, I haul him home.

My instinct for judging Yeager as an excellent horse works out well. He begins to trust me, soaking up my extra grooming and affection like a sponge. For several weeks I ride him at a relaxed pace on trails.

Then the first time I take him in an arena, no problem. He knows I won't hurt him. As I'd hoped, we win barrel races in various horse shows and rodeos.

For my last year of high school, I choose the Orme School located on a working ranch in Mayer, Arizona. What makes Orme perfect is taking Yeager to school with me. He has his own stall and a small corral. When I am selected as Rodeo Queen Attendant, I ride Yeager. And he does his best for me running in barrel races at the Orme Rodeo.

After graduating from high school, I keep Yeager in my parents' corral. I still help in the summer with stacking hay bales, feeding horses, and shoveling out the manure around the stable. A difficult decision comes when I go to college. If I'm not riding him anymore, I won't ask my parents to feed Yeager and shelter him. The time has come to sell my quarter horse gelding. Comet has already been loaned to a friend. The herd in the corral is dwindling. My life heads in a new direction.

After placing an ad for Yeager in the newspaper, I get a response from a young man. He wants to buy a horse for his father back East. He admires Yeager's beauty, disposition, and excellent confirmation. I tell him, "You can drive the wheels off your car before you'll find another horse as good as Yeager."

"He'd be perfect for my father. How much do you want for him?"

"Only $2,000," I say. The buyer doesn't hesitate, and writes me a check for the full asking price. At first I feel like a successful horse trader, having bought him for $500 and selling him for $2,000. Then I feel a lump in my throat because I will miss Yeager. We've had good times together and I have a deep affection for him. I stroke his warm neck. To say good-bye we sniff noses, taking in each other's breath. "Bye-bye, good friend," I whisper. "May it go well for you."

6

Beatletoast

6:10 a.m.

On July 26, waking me up out of a half sleep were the voices of Laurie Parsons and Gus Mircos on KOA radio. They bantered about the fact that memorabilia from Beatle George Harrison was being offered at an auction in London. The items included hard candy and a twenty-eight-year-old "piece of toast."

Half awake, I began thinking, *How would a person know to save his toast because he was going to be famous? Or did George Harrison's mother have a clutter problem and she just discovered it?*

I ferreted out my photo album and opened to the page about the Beatles. There was my blue admission ticket to the concert at Red Rocks Amphitheatre in Colorado. The ticket said: "KIMN presents THE BEATLES in concert/Admission $6.60/Date: August 26, 1964."

A snapshot my mother took of three cowgirls and three cowboys from Little Britches Rodeo standing by a white car sticks to the page. We looked so cool. For the Beatles we wore no cowboy hats or western clothes. Not for a Beatles concert! My long hair appeared to have been ironed and lightened in streaks with peroxide.

Next to the snapshot is a newspaper photograph of the Beatles getting off their chartered airplane at Stapleton International Airport. The caption reads: "The Beatles were greeted by a howling mob of 10,000 fans. After a swift journey by auto, they arrived at the Brown Palace Hotel where another mob of fans gave them a warm welcome."

I still remember seeing photos in magazines of all those crazy love-struck girls screaming and reaching out to the Beatles at their concerts. Those girls were totally emotional, I thought. No self-control. They were so uncool!

My friends and I arrived at Red Rocks before noon so we could get good seats on the flagstone slabs. We were excited and thrilled that we found a spot only twelve rows back from the stage. We were going to have a good view of this group that seemed larger than life.

The Righteous Brothers opened the concert. At exactly 9 p.m., the Beatles, wearing matching collarless suits, walked out in a line. John, Paul, and George picked up their guitars, and Ringo sat down behind the drums. The first song was "I Wanna Hold Your Hand." Hearing that song on the radio sure got me happy inside, and got me interested in the Beatles. I felt bubbly and high spirited. I wondered if there was any way to keep this experience from ending. The harmonies captivated me.

They continued to sing one hit after another: "All My Loving," "This Boy," and "I Saw Her Standing There."

By the time the Beatles sang about hearts going boom, the crowd was going crazy and screaming.

I struggled to control myself. *Keep this quiet, don't tell anyone, OK?* After "Love Me Do," I lost it. I felt a scream start and I just let it happen. I've never screamed with joy like that in my life. My friends screamed, too, all of us swept away with emotion. I felt exhilarated and on fire.

When the concert ended we wanted more. The night had enchanted us.

So now you know one of my secrets. I screamed at a Beatles concert. And I realize now it's good to let go once in a while, have a great time, and let the music take you away.

And I've learned that when I'm awakened to news of Beatletoast, some memories never die.

The Canyon Courier, August 14, 1991

Ticket from Beatles concert, August 26, 1964

7

Always the Hero

Dad is a lot of fun. He's seventy-seven, and the other day at 5:30 p.m., he said, "Would you and the kids like some ice cream?"

"It's too close to dinner," I remind him, but I understand his impulses. The priorities of my father are to be generous and to enjoy his life.

His attitudes may have been shaped partly by his experiences in World War II. He was a navigator on a B-24 Liberator bomber, which was shot down by the Japanese over the Celebes Islands.

The pilot, nose gunner, and bombardier were killed instantly. Dad and the top turret gunner had to push the panic-stricken copilot out of the plane and then jump out themselves, praying that their parachutes would open. They were less than eight hundred feet above the ocean when they bailed out.

Dad and the copilot were captured by a Japanese patrol boat, which took them to a prison camp, where Dad was beaten. Because he wouldn't give the Japanese information they wanted about the location of other American airmen, he was placed in front of a firing squad. They cocked their guns on three occasions, and each time Dad expected to die. For some reason his captors didn't shoot.

In prison camp Dad got down to one hundred pounds and could no longer stand up. The guards transferred him to another camp for severe cases, those prisoners who were expected to die. But British jewel thieves who were also prisoners in the new camp gave my starving father stolen crab and sugar. His health improved.

With the grace of God and the kindness of the British jewel thieves, Dad survived the war. And at the age of seventy-five, he received a belated Silver Star for exceptional bravery. A retired air force colonel had nominated him after learning that Dad had never been decorated.

My older brother had been born soon after Dad left for overseas duty in the South Pacific. I was born after Dad returned from World War II. Looking back, I consider my father an inspiration. In trials he looked out for the safety of his comrades, but he also took care of himself. Throughout his trials in prison, he had a strong spirit.

My mother told me, "Even though he was missing in action for two years, I always loved your father deeply and I had faith he would return. He was a survivor."

Her instincts proved accurate. He came back and after regaining his health, he set to work as the provider for our family.

Dad, who had grown up in Hoopeston, Illinois, majored in economics at Yale University. And with his outgoing personality he became quite successful in business. But with success and fatherhood came stress, and Dad found relief in drinking. He became an alcoholic, but none of us knew it by that name. My brother and I just knew it in the feelings we had, the tension and uneasiness when he was "over-served."

Dad found the strength to quit drinking when I was a freshman in college. He later told me, "I didn't like the hangovers, and I was afraid your mother would leave me if I didn't quit drinking. He also was upset about the last Thanksgiving dinner he had ruined. Somehow all those things clicked at once. He went to Alcoholics Anonymous.

Of all the things Dad has done, such as providing for us the way he did, the fun trips he took me on, his faith in me as a person, there is one thing I am most grateful for—that he quit drinking.

One wonderful service Dad has done over the years has been to help other alcoholics to get sober. He has been their sponsor and has taken them to meetings. He says, "Helping others is part of the program. That's how I stay sober."

Dad and Mom have been married almost fifty years, and they are enjoying their retirement together.

Our children have a grandfather who takes them fishing and watches their soccer games. They love it when he buys them ice cream.

And I have a father who I love and respect very much. He has taught me what is important about being alive.

The Chicago Tribune, June 21, 1992

4 SOUTHLAND CAPTIVES FREE

Names of four Southern Californians liberated from German prison camps and one freed from a Japanese camp were announced yesterday by the War Department. They Are:

Germany

NICHOLAS S. GANDOLFO Jr., Pvt.; mother, Mrs. Palmiera Gandolfo, Artesia.

EDWARD B. SOLTWEDEL, 2/Lt.; wife, Margaret, Huntington Park.

CLIFFORD B. STEWART, Pfc.; mother, Mrs. Dora Stewart, Gardena.

SAMUEL S. TURETSKY, S/Sgt.; mother, Mrs. Anna Turetsky, 2923 Bellevno avenue.

Japan

WILLIAM McFERREN, 1/Lt.; wife, Betty, Corona.

Bill McFerren (my Dad) released from Japanese Prison Camp, 1945

8

How Fishing Improves Your Vocabulary

Yesterday I hooked a fish. After putting up a good fight, he said, "I'm just floundering around."

"You're too young to talk," I said, and threw him back in the stream.

"Sucker," he shrieked.

"Fish should be seen and not heard!"

Besides instructing me about how to tell fish stories, my father attempted to teach me to bubble fly-fish years ago. In case you haven't had experience with this type of fishing, I will briefly explain what little I know. You obtain a rod with a spinning reel, and tie on a clear bubble, half filled with water. (It is recommended you not fall into the lake or stream while you are filling the bubble because this scares the fish.)

After you have filled the plastic bubble half full, you tie on the leader with the fly. Then you cast out your line into the lake or stream without hooking yourself or your fishing buddies. Hopefully your fly lands lightly on the water as if it were the real thing. Steady as a rock you reel back slowly—very slowly.

I assure you it's possible to cast out your bubble and fly thousands of times without catching a fish. This does not mean you are a bad person or that the fishing spirits are against you.

When the wind comes up and the line appears to be hopelessly tangled, the fun begins. You may use words you wouldn't say to your mother. Then as you work your fingers unknotting your line, your mind is free to wander. As I untangle lines for hours, I start thinking about vocabulary words I have torn off my daily calendar—and how they relate to fishing. Here are a few that come to mind:

Abulia: abnormal lack of ability to make a decision. Possibly the fish who circles your bait but doesn't bite is having a case of abulia.

Petard: a case containing explosives to break down a door or gate or breach a wall. If you throw a petard into the stream where you are fishing, you might be a redneck.

Cliometrics: application of methods developed in other fields to the study of history. As I attempt to straighten out my line, I realize that cliometrics might apply here. I must move my hook through the loops carefully to untangle my fishing line. This might apply to the U.S. Congress when members get tangled up.

Palpable: capable of being touched or felt. There is nothing like the palpable feeling of a fish on the line. It makes your heart thump with excitement.

Pastiche: hodgepodge. My tackle box looks like a pastiche of items from my junk drawer.

Celerity: rapidity of motion or action. A fish bites your fly, swims deep under the water, but with celerity breaks your line.

If a fish breaks my line, I sputter a four-letter word, just like my father did years ago.

Colorado Community Media newspapers, July 26, 2012

Mom and Dad in their fishing boat, 1983

Part Two

Shaking Off My Bridle

All things are bound together. All things connect.
—Chief Seattle

9

The Roots of My Newspaper Writing

The University of Colorado at Boulder rocks with unrest in the fall of 1966 due to American military involvement in the Vietnam War. As a CU college student, I feel the strain of the war. My brother, a pilot, flies for the navy in Vietnam, and my best friend's fiancé serves in the army.

In stark contrast to the ugliness of the war is the beauty of the Colorado University campus at the base of the Rocky Mountains. Heavy winds whoosh down across the Flatirons, enormous granite slabs perfect for rock climbing, just west of campus.

In 1966 the University of Colorado students run the newspaper *The Colorado Daily*. One day while scanning the paper, I notice an ad asking for student reporters with "no experience required." In the next hour, editor Bob Ewegen gives me a job as a reporter for the paper.

He first assigns me to cover the Candlelight Peace March, organized by a cross-country group that prays for an end to the Vietnam War. I interview the leader of the march, shoot a photograph of him, and write the story that the next day appears on the front page of the *Colorado Daily*.

When I see my first story in print with my byline, Mary McFerren, I feel buoyant. I'm a newspaper writer for a good paper. It doesn't seem to matter I'm not a journalism major because writing stories comes naturally for me. It helps that I'm curious about people and what makes them tick. When I ask questions, and the subject person answers, more questions bounce back from me. I find reporting and interviewing stimulating.

Besides editor Ewegen, I work with Pat McGraw. Many nights I stay up with other reporters and copy editors until 3 a.m. in the *Colorado Daily* office to get the paper out. We reporters create a racket typing triple space on clunky manual typewriters. The pounding gives evidence that we either are doing important work, knocking the walls down, or both.

Click, click, bang, bang, as we type, and ring, ding, ding as we manually yank the return shifts. The typewriters are metronomes, and we percussionists hold the beat.

One week David Chalfant, editor of *Ethos*, the creative weekly section of the newspaper, plans a trip. He assigns me to edit *Ethos* while he's away. But he doesn't leave me any copy, so I run a group of my own stories influenced by the writings of Beatle John Lennon's book *In His Own Write*. Later my conscience nags at me—should I have run my own work in the creative section? Too much ego?

No one criticizes.

In 1968 I transfer to Bard College, two hours north of New York City on the Hudson, to further my studies as an art major. I resemble a hippie with long curly hair and bell bottoms. When I arrive at the Bard campus in upstate New York near Woodstock, a student finds out I'm from Colorado. "You're from the land of cowboys and Indians," he says.

"You've got it, friend, I'm a cowgirl. Besides racing horses, I ride bucking steers."

"Oh, that explains the bowlegs."

I laugh. "Yeah, that explains it."

Colorado Community Media newspapers, December 2013

Me, a college student, 1967

10

Jack Klugman and Me

Jack Klugman, the movie star and television actor, died at age ninety in 2012, and I felt it personally. Ouch, I will miss him. I had firsthand experience with his kindness—and his unkempt tendencies. A "messy" in real life, it was natural for Jack Klugman to play Oscar the slob in the TV series The Odd Couple.

It seems like just yesterday I was a Bard College junior and landed my first job on a movie crew as a wardrobe manager for Who Says I Can't Ride a Rainbow! *The non-union film starred Jack Klugman as a generous "city cowboy" who runs a block-sized pony ranch in Lower Manhattan. In the movie, kids from Harlem visit Jack's menagerie and connect with animals. Jack's character teaches the kids responsibility through feeding, grooming, and cleaning up after the ponies.*

As I came from a one-acre ranch in Colorado, with horses, goats, and chickens, the story resonated with me.

It is January 1970, in New York City, and the actors' and film crew's headquarters occupy an unheated warehouse garage. When the shooting occurs outside, our breath looks like smoke. Brrr. My toes turn into icicles.

On the first day of shooting after the director says, "It's a wrap," Jack drops everything he is wearing to the floor of his dressing room, shimmies into his street clothes, and tears out of the garage. Yikes. I pick up his clothes from the floor and hang them up ready for the next day's shoot.

On the third day of production, the director presents me with a tan canvas coat lined with sheepskin. "Mary, could you make this new coat look old—like something Jack's character would wear?" he asks.

"Sure ... no problem!" I say.

I take the spanking new coat out to the horse corral and lay it in the dry refuse left behind by the ponies.

With my cowboy boots I stomp on the jacket until it has a patina of crud on it. *Now it looks like a real cowboy's coat.* After dusting it off, I proudly hang it in Jack Klugman's dressing room.

Moments later I hear screaming. "Who did this? How the h—— am I going to leave the set smelling like sh——?"

Apprehensive and trembling I approach Jack.

He glares at me.

Afraid I might be fired, I blurt out, "I am so sorry, but where I come from, smelling like horse debris is normal. Some call it prairie perfume."

"But this is New York City and I'm staying in an upscale hotel. They won't let me in if I come in stinking up the lobby!"

He must have thought I had turned his "coat of many colors" into a rag. I suppress a laugh.

What pleases me was instead of getting me fired, Jack learns my name. Every morning after the coat incident he says, "Hi, Mary." Maybe he thinks he'd better keep an eye on me and if we communicate we'll work better together—and we do.

Now forty-three years later, I read Jack Klugman's bestseller, *Tony and Me: A Story of Friendship.* In the book Jack explains he never trusted people or got close to them until he learned what a real friend was through working with Tony Randall on *The Odd Couple* television series. Maybe Jack Klugman saw I was a real person with good intentions after I trashed his coat on *Who Says I Can't Ride a Rainbow!* I suspect with all that bravado he exhibited, he was just covering up a soft heart.

I hope I have the pleasure of meeting Jack Klugman again in the great beyond. If I meet him, he'll say, "Hi, Mary," because it's rumored in heaven people remember each other's names.

"Hi, Jack," I'll say. "Here we are together again. What did you ever do with that coat?"

Colorado Community Media newspapers, February 2013

Jack Klugman and Me

By Mary Stobie

Jack Klugman, the movie star and television actor who passed away in December, was honored at this year's Academy Awards.

Jack Klugman

11

Sentimental

I attend my college reunion at Bard College in upstate New York. It already seems an eternity since I transferred in 1968 from the University of Colorado to Bard, a small liberal arts college, as an art major. During the reunion, a Sunday morning memorial service is held for classmates who died the previous year. One of the men from my class has died of AIDS.

One of my female classmates weeps openly for this man. I am surprised and touched by her tears. I realize I expect her to be cool and aloof, like my Bard adviser, whose attitude toward me colored my entire impression of the school—and, by extension, of the East Coast.

James Sullivan, a painter form New York City, was my adviser. When I applied to transfer to the art department, Sullivan looked at my portfolio of art and said disdainfully, "Sentimental."

Ouch! I changed my style for a while to New York contemporary— abstract, cold, and detached. Recognizable objects that bring up warm emotions were a no-no. I tried color field painting for a time, with no discernable shapes. The teachers and students said they liked my paintings. Hey, I wanted to fit in, be a successful artist. I was young enough to be concerned about the "in" style.

But inside I felt restless because it wasn't really my style of art I created—it was someone else's. A painter from Colorado cannot turn into a New York artist in twelve easy lessons.

After graduation, years passed. I dropped painting for photography— and New York for Colorado. My photography evolved from commercial jobs for the City of Denver and rodeo photography to family snapshots and portraits, with lots of subjects being children and pets. Maybe James Sullivan, my adviser, was correct after all. Maybe I am sentimental.

The reunion is combined with commencement. Bard alumnus Chevy Chase delivers the keynote speech. Laughing so hard my sides hurt, I almost fall off my chair.

At a small alumni party, I discover Chevy Chase's wife is a full-time mother. Several of my female classmates who attend the reunion are full-time mothers, too. One is a retired psychotherapist who had her kids later in life like me.

I discover not all my classmates went on to be successful artists or authors. Sure, some of the women are television actresses, doctors, and lawyers. But some of us are happy to put our skills, education, and intelligence into our families and children, and in my case write on the side while raising my kids.

Luckily my college adviser doesn't show up, so I don't have to think of what to say to him. And the woman who cries for the lost classmate friend who died of AIDS—she permits herself to show emotion, to be sentimental.

What a relief.

The Denver Post, November 1990

Bard College ten-year reunion with Chevy Chase, 1982

12

Rodeo Photographer

Spring, 1970

After the shock of learning about the Kent State shootings, I felt depressed and sad. Due to the campus unrest, Bard shut down for the rest of the school year, April and May. With no reason to be in New York, I moved back to Colorado. I felt grief about leaving New York, thinking my chances for fame and fortune were shot to bits. I was sure that returning to Colorado would be a letdown. But the first week back home in Golden, a girlfriend invited me to a rodeo in Grover, a small town in northern Colorado. Carrying my Pentax camera, I entered the arena and took action shots of professional cowboys riding broncs and bulls. The earth smelled excellent, like home. My boots felt comfortable on my feet. The earth, the sky, western people, and horses lifted me out of my depression.

I fell off, I got on again.

The rodeo contestants ask for copies of my photos. "Sure thing," I say. After setting up a darkroom in my parents' basement in Golden I am in business. At the next rodeo not only do I sell 8 × 10 prints to the cowboys, but also am hired as a photographer for the *Rodeo Sports News*.

National bareback bronco riding champion Chris Ledoux and five-time all-round-champion cowboy Larry Mahan compete professionally during this period. One of my best shots, which I frame and hang in my parents' kitchen, is of black cowboy Myrtis Dightman, a top bull rider.

At the Colorado State Fair in Pueblo, I position myself to take a photo of the next rider out of the bucking chutes. My boots are planted deep in the rancid dust, the "prairie perfume" of the rodeo arena. The sun beats down on my back as I squint through the viewfinder, ready to catch the action.

"No women allowed in the arena—get out!" a voice hollers from behind me. I whirl around. The stock contractor wearing mirrored sunglasses stands next to me mounted on a gargantuan horse.

While he distracts me from my photography work for the *Rodeo Sports News*, a loose bucking horse knocks me down and gallops over me. Holy smokes! Two inches either way and he would have stepped on my back or head. I was inches from death.

Shaken up from being run over, and knowing I could have been seriously injured, I wish I could kick the stock contractor's ass. Muttering complaints, I climb out of the arena with my camera covered with dust.

What the chauvinistic schmuck doesn't know or care about is that I've photographed rodeos all over Colorado. When I stand in the arena near the chutes at rodeos, the best spot for a photographer, no other stock contractor harasses me. My favorite stock contractor, jovial Harry Vold, is nicknamed "The Duke." Where is Vold when I need him?

A reporter from the *Pueblo Chieftain*, Grace Lowe, sees what happened. She interviews and photographs me and writes an article for the *Chieftain* titled "Liberation Day a Dud for Golden Girl at Fair." (She refers to women's liberation, which commands much attention in the news.) Lowe astutely writes a timely story about my experience at the Colorado State Fair and connects it to women's liberation.

I don't think of my work as "liberated"; I just think I'm using my skill with photography. But the rodeo boss may see me as a threat to his bucking events, or as Lowe writes in her article, he might be trying "to protect" me. If his reason is to protect me, he sure makes a mess of it, almost getting me killed!

Whatever his reasons for kicking me out of the arena, the contractor can't stop me from working. I continue to photograph rodeos for several years. When the boss who won't allow women in the arena contracts a rodeo such as Cheyenne Frontier Days, I stand on the roof of the grandstand with a long lens and shoot the rodeo action from above. As a rodeo photographer, I do what I have to do.

The Miller Stockman Art Gallery in Denver hangs a selection of my framed rodeo photographs, along with Charlie Russell's paintings and other western artists. I sell a few. Although I like shooting stills of rodeo action, the movie business is still in my blood from working in New York *City on Who Says I Can't Ride a Rainbow!* with Jack Klugman. On a movie set I feel connected with other creative people, both in the cast and on the crew. I miss that.

Colorado Community Media newspapers, November 2013

Postcard with my photo, 1972

13

The Honkers

In 1972, an ad in the Rodeo Sports News *caught my eye: "Film producer hiring cowboys for a Hollywood movie to be filmed in New Mexico. Call 213-444-9500."*

Because I'd worked on a movie in New York, I called the production manager to ask for a job. He hired me over the phone to help in wardrobe for The Honkers. *Excited with the prospect of working on a movie again, I packed a suitcase and headed my pickup truck south toward Carlsbad, New Mexico.*

When I arrive in Carlsbad, I drive to the rodeo arena, the set for the movie *The Honkers*. (A honker is a bull or bronc that can't be broken.) My favorite stock contractor, Harry Vold, actor James Coburn, actor Slim Pickens, and five-time world-champion cowboy Larry Mahan are all at the rodeo arena. Because I already know Vold and Mahan, I feel right at home. I'm dressed western, wearing a leather belt with a buckle I won with Yeager in barrel racing.

From the beginning, this movie crew, including Steve Lodge, cowriter of the screenplay who runs the wardrobe department, has good chemistry. We work mostly outdoors and are comfortable around horses and bucking stock. Steve Ignat, the director of *The Honkers* and his pregnant wife, Sally, set the tone, both friendly and down to earth. Ignat suffers with migraines, and I give him Midol. He says it helps.

During production of *The Honkers*, leading man, trim gray-haired James Coburn always appears on time for the shoot. I observe that he works twelve-hour days without a complaint. I'm impressed with his work habits and calm, collected demeanor.

Talk about connection—many of this cast and crew feel like family. Slim Pickens, who plays the rodeo clown in the movie, makes me smile every time I see him. Maybe it's because of his unique speaking voice, friendliness, and sense of humor. Somewhere in my things I have a tape of him singing a song for me he made up, "I'm a Rodeo Cowboy."

Director Ignat asks me to double for Anne Archer, who plays the love interest to James Coburn. I stand at the top of a hill above the rodeo arena with my hair blowing in the wind. My next assignment as her double is to drive a red Pantera, the sexiest sports car I've ever ridden in. As I help Anne Archer with wardrobe, I loan her my personal turquoise jewelry to wear in the movie.

The shop owners in the small town of Carlsbad treat those of us working on the movie as if we are kings and queens, which surprises me. I guess it isn't every day so much excitement comes to the Carlsbad, New Mexico, known for the caverns full of bats.

When *The Honkers* wraps up on location, I consider my options for continuing to work on movies. Except for the cowboys, the cast and crew will all return to Hollywood. Before we all split up, still photographer Orlando Suero hands me his business card. "Look me up if you visit Hollywood," he says.

I slip his card into my wallet. "You'll see me soon."

The Honkers cast and crew. Top row, left to right: Steve Ignat, Slim Pickens, Harry Vold, Mary (McFerren) Stobie, Larry Mahan, James Coburn, Floyd Daze. Bottom row, left to right: Gene Talvin, Ross Dollarhyde, Steve Lodge, Elliott Schick.

Part Three

Lassoing Fame

Certain things catch your eye, but pursue only those that capture your heart.
—Old Indian saying

Mary McFerren

14

Meeting Warren Beatty

When I first moved to Hollywood, I sublet an apartment in foggy Santa Monica near the ocean, a stucco one-bedroom apartment with geraniums and succulents in the garden by my door.

Within days of settling in, I dial the pink wall phone in the kitchen.

"Hi, Orlando, it's Mary McFerren. I'm in town. Remember me from working in wardrobe on *The Honkers*?"

"Mary! Of course I remember you. Stop by and see me on the set of *Shampoo* in Beverly Hills," he says, and gives me the address of Mildred Pierce restaurant on La Cienega Boulevard in Beverly Hills.

I take extra care to look my best and wear an aqua knit top, gray-striped jeans, and red cowboy boots. I brush out my long golden brown hair before I climb into my green Karmann Ghia.

Movie lights are set up on the patio of the restaurant; the crew works with cables. The 35 mm movie camera sits like a sphinx, the center of the action. I make an entrance onto the set of *Shampoo*, a movie about a top Hollywood hairdresser who plays musical beds with his girlfriends.

Orlando, a short jovial man wearing a vest with pockets for camera accessories and three Nikon cameras hanging from his neck, greets me warmly.

Within moments, the director and star of *Shampoo* is standing in front of me, close. It's Warren Beatty, so near I can smell his aftershave.

Beatty gazes into my eyes. His animal magnetism overwhelms me. My mind scrambles. I'm the hot-blooded young woman who screamed at a Beatles concert. *Don't lose it.*

When I was thirteen my parents took me to see *Splendor in the Grass,* a love story starring the man in front of me and Natalie Wood. Beatty played Bud, the sexy teenager—he and Natalie Wood heated up the movie theater with their chemistry.

Now I'm the one on fire. Beatty is still looking straight into my eyes. I am tongue-tied and, surprisingly, Beatty also lacks the gift of gab.

Let's fly to Ireland, Warren, you and me, and kiss the Blarney Stone. To loosen our tongues.

"Warren, this is Mary McFerren," Orlando interjects. "We worked together with Jimmy Coburn and Anne Archer on *The Honkers.* Mary did wardrobe."

Beatty's expression cools. He takes a step back.

Wardrobe, damn it. I chew my lip and watch him. Without a word he ambles off.

The movie star's hypnotic spell over me dissipates.

"Hey, wait a minute, Warren," I say. "Come back. I'm a cowgirl from Colorado and I can teach you how to ride a bull!"

Orlando chuckles. "She really can, Warren," he says. "I saw her ride a steer on *The Honkers.*" Orlando and I visit a few minutes before he leaves to take photographs for the movie.

I call my mother later and tell her everything.

"Warren Beatty?" she says, impressed. "What was he like?"

"Very nice-looking, but shy and awkward. Kind of a geek."

Geek, my eye. I didn't tell her what I was really thinking.

Beatty may have thought he'd never see that "wardrobe woman" friend of Orlando's again. But the forces of the universe decided Beatty and I weren't off the hook with each other yet.

Six months later, Christmas day, I find myself at Warren Beatty's house in the Hollywood Hills. It's 1974 and the Vietnam War is still raging. Nixon has resigned.

Warren is dating Michelle Phillips of The Mamas and the Papas fame. By now I, too, have a boyfriend, Peter Pilafian, who is somehow related to Michelle. This relationship puts us, at one o'clock Christmas afternoon, at the front door of Warren Beatty's art deco home.

Beatty opens the door. He wears a satin bathrobe, which catches me by surprise. Did we get him out of bed? I feel overdressed in a long green skirt and dressy sleeved blouse. "Merry Christmas, come on in," he says. Wow! He can talk! I hadn't been so sure after our last encounter.

Beatty, in post-production for *Shampoo*, soon busies himself in conversation with screenwriter Robert Towne on the couch. I chat with Michelle Phillips. I admire her porcelain skin, pretty eyes, and long hair. She is friendly to me and seems kind as we talk about children. I wonder if Beatty will marry her.

Around six or seven Michelle and I are in the kitchen getting dinner ready. Michelle heats up frozen peas and I stir the mashed potatoes. A turkey bakes in the oven. Warren appears, still in his satin bathrobe. I say, "We're not serving breakfast. Warren, are you getting dressed for dinner?"

Beatty doesn't answer. Does it cost him a hundred dollars a word to talk?

At dinner he … wears his bathrobe.

I sip my wine. *Loosen up, Mary, and accept this man's ways in his own home.*

I am quickly learning, in just this one evening, to relax my own social style and have more fun. After all, I said I wanted adventure, and this sure feels like one.

When Peter and I leave Beatty's house after dinner, I thank him and Michelle for a lovely dinner. Warren says to me with a twinkle in his eye, "Mary, is your offer still open to teach me how to ride a bull?"

I crack up. "You betcha, Warren," I say.

Silent, green-robed waters run deep.

March, 1974

Actress in Hollywood composite shot, 1975

15

Hollywood Movie Star

Talk about tension. I had my fifteen minutes of fame when I appeared in a feature movie from Columbia Pictures called *Hardcore* in 1978. I had a speaking part in a scene with George C. Scott.

How did this come to be? How did a rodeo cowgirl from Colorado become nearly famous? You see, in my twenties I had delusions of grandeur. A palm reader had once studied my palm and told me the lines beneath my ring finger formed a star. This meant I would be a well-known person, or at least notorious.

So as many hopeful young twenty-somethings do, I moved to Hollywood to chase my dream. I wanted to re-create the creative synergy and sense of community I felt working on *Who Says I Can't Ride a Rainbow!* and *The Honkers*. I hoped moving to Hollywood would provide more projects like that and I would become famous in the process.

My original goal was to become a screenwriter. Based on a comedic screenplay I wrote called *Working for Nothing*, the American Film Institute in Beverly Hills accepted me as a "Screenwriting Fellow." As "fellows" in an exclusive film school at Greystone Mansion in Beverly Hills, we all had the chance to rub shoulders with famous actors, directors, and producers.

Paul Schrader, who wrote *Taxi Driver*, delivered a lecture for writers, which I attended. He mentioned a small seminar he was offering for ten students and accepted me into the class. He was an awesome teacher, who encouraged me by comparing my writing to the work of Preston Sturges. Schrader gave the class tips like, "Build tension and bring in the gun by page thirty of your screenplay."

At the time of the seminar, Schrader was in pre-production for *Hardcore* with George C. Scott. My improvisation acting class teacher said I was strong on stage, so I asked Schrader if I could read for a part in his movie.

"Who do you want to play?" he asked.

"The counter woman who George C. Scott talks with while placing an ad at the *Los Angeles Free Press*."

"Yes, call my casting director."

I read the part in the script for the casting director, Vic Ramos, got hired, and obtained a Screen Actors Guild card. My happy dancing down the sidewalk of Hollywood Boulevard attracted attention. Now what would I wear? *Hardcore* had a dark underbelly involving criminals, murderers, and sex, so I played against that by wearing my hair in pigtails and a red T-shirt that said "Mischief." I practiced my lines over and over until I had them down pat.

When I arrived at the set, I spotted George C. Scott—bigger and taller than I imagined. He sat in a director's chair with his huge mastiff dog sitting beside him like a sentry. Scott emanated power and all I could think of was General George Patton. I was a soldier facing a firing squad.

"The assistant director will run through your lines with you," director Paul Schrader told me. "George won't do it."

Yikes. Scott was too famous, too big a star, to rehearse with me. He was General George Patton in charge of the whole army of the crew, actors, even the director. In addition to the residue of General Patton in his spirit, Scott was now playing Jake Van Dorn, an angry, explosive father. He was fully in character and his dog stood at attention a few feet away, ready to attack me if I threatened his master.

To add to my nervousness, the male actor ahead of Scott in line at my counter said his line for his classified ad, "... fastest tongue in the West." I pictured his tongue running ahead of him down the road.

Then the gigantic George C. Scott took his place at the counter. As a wet-behind-the-ears actress facing this legend of an actor shadowed by his threatening dog, I felt jittery. I thought of Schrader's lesson in screenwriting class and bringing in the gun to create tension. I wanted to scream, "Enough tension, Paul Schrader, you punk film director!"

But instead, my throat tightened and I flubbed my line.

Scott glared at me and repeated my line to me. He was running circles around me! My face felt hot, as I was embarrassed. All eyes of the crew, and director, were focused on me.

Somehow I rose to the occasion and we completed the scene. I guess Paul Schrader liked my performance, because he gave me a close-up in the final cut. At the Hollywood screening debut of *Hardcore* for the cast, Schrader said to me, "You look good on screen and were very natural, Mary."

I was paid $275 for a few minutes of screen time and received enormous residuals of $10 a year. This was for *Hardcore* showings on movie channels, which helped my M&M's habit.

Appearing in *Hardcore* taught me three important things. First, you have to ask for what you want. I asked for the part and got it. Second, if you do anything in a movie, but especially acting, people think you are larger than life—superhuman and a little divine. Third, after these same people get to know you, as they did me, they come to suspect you are just a human being. At the same time they wonder if you will return to the screen.

Yes, I will. If given the chance, I will choose the risk, fun, and excitement of acting in a movie again.

Acting with George C. Scott in *Hardcore*, 1979

16

Monument Valley, Utah: Rock Climbing with Clint Eastwood's Gang

I didn't move to Hollywood in my twenties to learn to climb rocks with ropes, but I guess you could say I learned the ropes in more ways than one. My boyfriend, Peter, was an expert climber. He taught me how to do technical rock climbing. Because he had so much experience climbing, I felt secure following him on the ropes. Even when I couldn't see him, I trusted that he was waiting up ahead of me.

Due to Peter's reputation as both a climber and a soundman, he landed a job on Clint Eastwood's movie *The Eiger Sanction*. (Eastwood both starred in and directed the movie.) They shot some of the film in Switzerland, home of the real Eiger mountain, then traveled to Monument Valley, Utah, to film scenes involving a climbing school headed up by actor George Kennedy's character.

On set, in addition to working the camera and sound equipment, Peter and his close friend on the project, cameraman Mike Hoover, set up ropes and pitons for Eastwood to do his own stunts. Peter told me that in Switzerland Clint Eastwood was very agile, taking obvious risks on the rocks while commanding the actors and the crew.

Peter invited me to join him in Monument Valley, a majestic wonderland of bright sun, blue skies, red dirt, and rock steeples. Before shooting commenced, I climbed rocks with Peter, Hoover, and Hoover's girlfriend.

As a group we did some free climbing. I wore special rock climbing boots with Vibram soles, and clambered up granite crevices, cracks, and rock faces. The beauty of Monument Valley intoxicated and invigorated me with the common sight of Navajo Indians riding painted ponies through the red sandy canyons. It felt like we had entered another time, another world, when life was still primitive, lived outdoors, and bound to the earth.

The pure air, the rock steeples, and even the Hollywood film crew—led by a highly competent movie star director—convinced me I was at the center of the world. And I'll admit I loved the adrenaline rush of taking risks.

Early one morning before shooting begins, Hoover, his girlfriend, Peter, and I ride in a helicopter straight up to the top of a rock steeple. After circling and then pausing on top of the steeple, the pilot waits for us to exit without turning off the engine. Carrying ropes and bags of equipment, we hop out. Within seconds the chopper blasts straight up, the wind from the propellers whipping my hair around my face.

Peter and Hoover set up a Tyrolean Traverse, which involves ropes stretched between two rock steeples with more than a thousand feet of exposure. To accomplish the traverse across the rope, you sit in a harness and pull yourself along from one steeple to another.

Careful to stay away from the edge of the giant steeple we are planted on, I glance down at the ground below. A Navajo rider on a pony looks like a tiny ant moving through the red sand. I feel dizzy and back up further from the edge.

All three of my companions do the traverse, both ways. Then Peter says, "Mary, it's your turn."

"Are you ready, Mary?" Hoover asks.

As the pressure mounts, my heart pounds. Climbing with my hands and feet on granite handholds and footholds are one thing, but for me it would be sheer terror to hang from ropes suspended in the air. What if the ropes or equipment breaks, or what if I panic in the middle and can't get all the way across? I suddenly remember that an experienced climbing guide died on the Eiger in Switzerland at the beginning of shooting.

"Mary, come on," Peter urges.

Even though I desperately want to impress Peter and Hoover, and know I'd feel exhilarated if I accomplished the Tyrolean Traverse, I pause. My inner voice cries out like a bass drum in a marching band, "No, no, no! Don't do it."

I listen.

So much for the adrenaline rush. Survival instinct triumphs.

Learning the ropes in Hollywood sometimes means staying off of them.

Summer, 1974

Clint Eastwood on location in Monument Valley

In Monument Valley, me climbing on location of
The Eiger Sanction, 1974

17

Screamer for *Rocky*

It's 1975. I'm a Screenwriting Fellow, and part of a gaggle of thirty film students at the exclusive American Film Institute in Beverly Hills at Greystone Mansion. John Avildsen, the director of the movie *Rocky*, screens an unfinished "rough cut" of the film with Sylvester Stallone and Talia Shire for our class. I love the movie right away, even in unfinished form. As Sylvester Stallone runs through the streets with all that victory music, "getting stronger, getting stronger," I want to jump out of my seat and run with him.

Well, I don't get to stride next to him, but I do scream for him—for evermore.

After the screening, it turns out John Avildsen finds he needs to fill in the sound track for the big fight scene between Rocky and Apollo Creed. He turns again to AFI students, offering us an invitation to come to the sound studio and yell and scream for the sound track as if we were in the crowd at the fight. You bet I volunteer.

OK, to actually discern my voice in the crowd in the movie, you need the extraordinary hearing of a bat-eared-fox.

Or you're my mother.

My mother claimed she could hear me scream in the crowd when she watched the movie. Don't all mothers do that—recognize their own child's screams and wails?

In addition to admiring my vocal abilities, my mother was starstruck, and awed, when I began dating said *Rocky* director John Avildsen. She always watched the Academy Awards ceremony on television.

When she visited me in Hollywood at my house in Laurel Canyon and John Avildsen drove up in a red convertible to pick me up for a date, Mom looked impressed and radiant. John didn't mind when my mother took photos of him with her Instamatic camera.

Ah, John. A talented director. Pretty cute for a short guy, with blond hair and blue eyes. And a bit of a rascal, but that's another story. He had that combination of confidence and vulnerability that can be so attractive. He lamented to me ultra-sincerely, "I don't know where my next job is coming from or if I'll ever work again."

"Ah, Schnooki," I would say, surprised that a man of his talent would have serious doubts about his career. "After *Rocky* is released, you'll work a lot."

Job insecurity, of course, runs rampant in the film business and is one of the hazards of unemployment between film projects. Directors don't even have security on the job: A director can be fired by a producer in the middle of a movie, right on the set, because a higher-up suddenly wants him gone, for reasons real or imagined. Directors are in charge of the actors and the crew, but producers rule the roost by controlling the money.

As a writer, actor, and screamer, I felt plenty insecure myself in Hollywood. Hired, laid off, and hired again. The in-between project time can make you lose sleep.

But it sure impressed my mom, watching the Academy Awards in Colorado. *Rocky* snapped up an Oscar for Best Picture and John Avildsen claimed the Oscar for Best Director.

Mom said, "To think you went on a date with an Academy Award–winning director. Mary, you never cease to amaze me."

Part Four

A Herd of My Own

*Remember that your children are not your own,
but are lent to you by the Creator.*
—Mohawk proverb

Working in movies, performing stand-up comedy, and acting with George C. Scott created fond memories. But a more life-changing experience in Hollywood involved marrying Mike, a country western drummer I met in a comedy class. Two years after our wedding, I gave birth to our first baby. I had never known love like I felt for my squalling daughter, Lily.

To give her a better life, we sold our house on Waring Avenue, across from Paramount Studios. We moved to Evergreen, a mountain town just west of Denver.

The local paper, the Canyon Courier, *hired me as a writer. Thus I began my career as a newspaper columnist.*

18

Family Is Where the Love Is

In 1977, my older brother, Bill, an ex-navy flight commander, and I warmed ourselves by the fire in my father's cabin near Kenosha Pass in Colorado. I was thirty and still single, and my brother expressed concern about my lifestyle.

"You're a feminist—you want to avoid marriage," he said.

"No, I don't, but I'm not in a hurry," I said.

"You're over twenty-five."

"So are you. Why don't you get married?"

"I will when I meet the right woman."

"I suppose if I met a good man I'd think about it."

"You should think about having children."

"Why?"

"Your biological clock is ticking."

"Oh, give me a break."

"Family is where the love is," he said finally.

Although I was uncomfortable with his pressure, I knew he was right. It was difficult to hear because I didn't have any man in my life who I would have considered marrying.

Soon after this conversation, wedding bells rang for me. My brother, who spoke about the love in a family, remained a bachelor.

The value of family became an issue in the recent presidential elections, and there was a struggle for definitions of "family values."

Everyone wanted to get into the act, and opinions flew back and forth in political speeches and across newspaper editorial pages. I gave it some thought and realized that I believe that most of us have family values.

Ask anyone around town what they did for Christmas and usually they will say they spent it with family. We seek out our relatives at that time of year no matter whether we are single or married, parents or childless. We draw together.

Bill came over for a visit when my two kids were young. He brought a box of chocolates as a gift, and it was good to see him. I was making grilled cheese sandwiches and tomato soup for lunch.

"You have a wonderful family," he said.

"Thanks.

"But kids are a lot of work—all the meals you have to fix."

I thought about his statement and realized that I did fix a lot of meals—three a day, plus snacks and cleanup. My brother was right—he was always right. For a moment I felt doubtful about what I was doing.

"It is work but I enjoy it," I said.

Although he liked being with his niece and nephew, I could see he was glad he was single and free of all the responsibility of children. Some people are just meant to be bachelors. But I was sure he had mixed feelings about not sharing his life with anyone. He might have been lonely.

Family is where the love is, I thought to myself. But I didn't speak the words out loud to my brother as he had to me years ago.

It was something better felt than expressed.

The Canyon Courier, January 1993

Brother Bill, U.S. Navy Pilot, 1970

19

Becoming a Soccer Mom

I used to see glassy-eyed mothers hunching over the steering wheels of their four-wheel-drive vehicles on their way to their children's soccer practice.

They told me how they sometimes drove fifteen hundred miles a month, many of these miles going to soccer practices and soccer camps. Weekends swept these mothers away to soccer games outside of town, and tournaments in Wyoming and New Mexico.

I pitied these mothers. My children were preschoolers and I still had time to write.

But what's a mother to do if she finds a little athlete sprouting up in her family who never naps and is going full speed between 6:30 a.m. and 8:30 p.m.?

She must do something to channel that energy with boys and girls who are not content with throwing basketballs around the living room, running through the house with water balloons, or carving their names with forks into the furniture. We mothers have compared notes, and this is the truth.

We can't just say, "Go out in the street and play ball with the neighborhood kids." There aren't any baseball or basketball games on the block anymore like there were when I was a kid.

A table in front of the supermarket carries a sign that says "Soccer Registration." I pick up a flier titled "Soccer: Fun for the Whole Family." Visions of boys kicking balls fly through my head. The coach wants to sign up my five-year-old son, who asks, "Mom, can I play?"

Soccer is teamwork, I think to myself. My kid will learn teamwork. I'm about to break down when it occurs to me that my writing schedule will be obliterated if I sign the registration.

And Saturdays—when we can breathe a little, have people over, or even go away for the weekend—will be changed. There will be at least two months of booked Saturdays, plus afternoon practices in the fall and spring. Some of the practices will be at quite a distance.

Besides the driving issue, I've heard about overly competitive parents interfering at games, trying to coach from the sidelines. Would I become such a parent?

I'm looking at this soccer form and thinking how I want to raise a healthy kid, not a couch potato. I want my kid to have good self-esteem. But then I remember if my child takes to soccer, it could be a ten-year-commitment.

Maybe I'll go to a few soccer games and see my child's well-being change for the better. Maybe he'll get a good coach. Maybe he'll be a good player. And maybe I'll begin to adjust to the soccer schedule and say, "Hey, this is all right. Soccer's OK. Soccer is fun."

"Mom, I need to play." We're still standing at the table.

"We should talk to your father."

"He already said 'yes' last night at dinner."

I am caught.

"Well ... OK," I say.

"Yahoo! Soccer! Yahoo!" he says.

I swallow hard, fill out the registration, pay the fee, and walk into the market.

When I get into my car after grocery shopping, I hunch over the steering wheel and my eyes begin to glaze. I am looking forward to the first game. Just call me a team player. Yahoo.

The Chicago Tribune, April 5, 1992

20

Dare to Be Disorganized

Fall looms over us and with it the pressure to get organized. Books, articles, and lectures abound on how to get your act together. But what if you are hopelessly disorganized and you love it? Like me. I adore chaos. Perfectly dressed people make me nervous. Neat rooms make me uptight, and I refuse to get into neurotically clean cars. There's a lot of pressure on us messy types to clean up. You have to have your wits about you if you are going to avoid conforming to the standards of the masses.

One of the first rules for maintaining your disorder: Do not clean up for company! The pressure of cleaning up for visitors is a hard one to resist. Most of us are afraid to let people see how we really live. We must let go of this fear if we are to maintain disorder. The way we really are is fine. Why should we put on a front for someone? Would that someone mess up his or her house if he or she knew we were coming to visit and that we prefer clutter? Not on your life!

When any visitor walks in, there can be newspapers, half empty cups of coffee, and toys everywhere. If the guest needs to sit down, you can put the cushions back on the sofa or clear off a chair if you can find one.

If you're having a dance, you can get a snowblower and blow everything off the floor and into the corner. People will always remember your parties and the sparkle in your eyes because you painted a picture instead of cleaning up.

Your appearance? Now here's where you really can let your individuality show. Most people are terrified to be seen with non-brushed hair, a shirt half tucked in, or mismatched socks or shoes.

Not you. Some of my best hairstyles "happen" when I wake up in the morning. A night's sleep can do wondrous tricks with my locks—sections of hair flip off the top of my head and capricious strands jut off the side of my face.

Who wants to be seen with a smooth beauty-shop look? You'll look like a million other dull people. Wrinkled clothes? No problem. As long as they're clean. I don't even own an iron. That is the most ridiculous time-waster sold to humanity. The exterior of your house? First of all, if you're stuck with a lawn—don't mow it! Let it get long and full of flowering weeds. This will give your place character. Don't be brainwashed into short is beautiful. If you must have a short lawn, get a goat.

Your car? Now some people get more panicky about their automobile's appearance than anything else. Not a fingerprint allowed anywhere. Not a spot of dust on the dash or a speck of dirt on the windshield. Vanity.

You have to be determined to hold your disorder here. A few branches hanging off your bumper, which is covered with outdated bumper stickers, can show how you feel about order. When you drive through the mud, the more splatters the better. Consider it decoration.

Your schedule? You don't have one. When you wake up you have no idea what you're doing that day or even what day it is. The day's events build like a tornado.

It's lots of fun. You don't know whether you're going to the gym, the supermarket, or bonkers. How do you get things cluttered if you are naturally organized but feel too rigid and want to change?

1. When you're done with something, never put it away.

2. If you have small children, let them have access to every drawer and shelf in the house.

3. Don't write anything down—doctor's appointments, weddings, funerals, etc. Just remember what you want to remember.

4. When you're knee-deep in clutter and neck-deep in chaos, invite twenty people over for dinner.

So now you've made the change. Disorder is your middle name. Welcome to the club.

The Canyon Courier, August 8, 1985

21

On Entering the Mysterious World of ... Science

Science has never been my thing. The only memory I have about being a student of science was in ninth-grade biology class—dissecting a frog.

Yuk.

In high school I avoided courses such as chemistry and physics. Uncomfortable with the thought of those subjects, I stuck to English, math, drama, art, and history. In college, I didn't socialize with science majors. I hung out with the journalism, art, and philosophy crowd.

Now I'm afraid that if they scanned my brain, the part that is used for science would cause consternation. "Tsk-tsk, look at that atrophy," they would say. "You're a perfect example of the old axiom: 'If you don't use it, you lose it.'"

Oops. I'm a parent now, and when my kids reach elementary school, those science fair packets start coming home every year. I scan them and quickly realize that if I don't understand the instructions, and if my stomach knots up just holding the blasted things, then science fair is to be avoided at all costs. For a few years I get away with it. Until this year. Suddenly both of our kids really want to be in the science fair and they both have a topic and a question.

"When are we going to start our science projects?" they both ask incessantly.

"Uh … um … uh …" I utter. My husband, with a business and music background, remains stone silent. But the kids grab our arms. "Come on, let's get started," they chorus.

The kids catch their father and me like two sparrows in a net. How could we deny our kids this academic challenge that they want to embark upon? Our numbers are up. I hear a voice from above: *Hey, you two slackers. Don't you know I built this entire world using scientific principles?*

"OK, OK, we'll do science fair," I say. My husband reluctantly agrees to help with one of the projects.

For the first time, having two kids doing science projects, which would be judged with ribbons and put on public display, brings a new level of stress into our home. For our kids to commit to this size of a project, with eight pages of instructions, they need my husband's and my assistance. Forming a hypothesis (it's all Greek to me), conducting an experiment (the fun part), and trying to figure out terms from the instructions like "control group," "experimental group," "independent variable," and "dependent variable" challenges all of us.

I clench my teeth.

We help the kids obtain materials for their displays, set up a computer schedule so they could take turns, and sacrifice the dining room table to permanent mess during the month before the science fair.

A mother dropping her kids off at the elementary school has dark circles under her eyes.

"Science fair getting to you?" I ask.

"Right, my husband and I fight over the science fair!" she says.

I love friends who will be that honest. Why, I observed, is it the parents, not the kids, who get stressed out? Is it the judging and competition that reflects back on us?

After sacrificing many Saturdays of skiing, my husband says, "This is the last time I'm doing this."

The science fair deadline approaches like a thunderstorm. The kids finish their displays, complete their notebooks. We help them carry the whole kit and caboodle over to school. Our son's project, "How Does a Nuclear Bomb Work?" is displayed in the gym. Our daughter's "What Makes People Ticklish?" is displayed in the library.

Phew.

Of course at that point, kids and parents feel a rush of accomplishment, having completed an important project. Mike and I have a realization that science fair creates a valuable learning experience with a final product, and not so bad after all.

The Canyon Courier, March 24, 1993

22

Tales of Lake McConaughy

Often I feel too busy as a mother and crave a life with more quality. So, while my husband, Mike, and our son, Jim, do three youth sporting events over a Memorial Day weekend, my daughter, Lily, twelve years old, and I shed schedules and pressure. We head for the sunshine and sandy beaches of Lake McConaughy, Nebraska.

As we drive northeast on Interstate 76 through eastern Colorado, the vistas open up. The mountain forests of home and traffic congestion of Denver are replaced by open farmland, wide prairie, and a grand blue sky. The strip of freeway stretches to the horizon. As we drive further east in Colorado, I comment to my daughter, "Look at that skyline— no housing developments, no telephone poles."

"Truly exquisite," she says.

We stop for gas at a Sinclair station with a statue of a green dinosaur next to the gas pumps. I fill the car with gas and then go inside to fill my travel mug with coffee. When I go to pay, the older lady behind the counter says. "The gas is $13.24 but the coffee is on the house."

I grin. "Thanks so much."

We have only driven a hundred miles from the Denver metro area, but I already feel animated. The feeling of freedom builds as we intersect with Interstate 80 and head east. In Nebraska we exit at the town of Ogallala and then drive across the dam to the north shore of Lake McConaughy.

I'm glad I'm driving a four-wheel-drive vehicle, as no roads exist along the beach. Motorboats create waves, which lap up on the deep sand. Even though we meet a group of campers from our church, no schedule hampers us. Soon we find a few friends who arrived early. While Lily and I unpack our tent, we see our friends have graduated to campers. A competent male friend kindly helps us level our spot and set up the tent under a cottonwood tree. A warm dry wind rattles the leaves.

Some people avoid the beach because they don't like sand in their food. I adjust and make myself forget what a cheese sandwich on white bread would taste like without grit. Saturday is a day that Taffy, our lazy cat, would respect. I lie in the sun, visit with friends, and barely prepare food. Lily romps with a group of other kids her age— she swims, learns to windsurf, and rides an inner tube towed around the lake by a motorboat. My most active moment is riding as a passenger in a friend's motorboat for a spin around the lake. My ambition level drops to zero. I don't open my book. If I slow down more, I'll turn into melted butter.

Besides happy campers, the symbol of Lake McConaughy for me is the dogs—assorted mutts wearing scarves, happy as clams running in the surf. I resonate with their free, joyful "life is good" selves. One dripping German Shepherd rolls and shakes sand all over me after I have just applied suntan oil. I barely react because I am too relaxed and the dog is too happy.

I love the spirit of the dogs that weekend, big or little, every last one of them.

Each dog has a smile on its face. Lily and I are not the only ones who like to escape the helter-skelter of modern life.

The dogs run free at Lake McConaughy.

And so do we.

The Canyon Courier, June, 1994

23

Day on the Prairie

When my son was a third-grader, his class and a few parent volunteers like me wore headbands and pretended we were Native Americans for the day.

It all felt very strange. The kids needed to learn about the enigmatic, self-sufficient people who inhabited this area for so long; so did the parents. But with every lesson, I felt the absence of the people themselves, innocents who our forbearers had decimated in horrific ways.

Third-graders in Jefferson County act out Native American life during the annual "Day on the Prairie." Children are divided into tribes, and parent volunteers are matched up with the kids and called "Wise Ones."

Many of the Wise Ones, including me, researched the Native Americans a bit in advance. I learned that in the second half of the 1800s, Colorado citizens tried to get rid of all the "Indians." And, in 1864, the U.S. Calvary slaughtered more than a hundred peaceful Cheyenne and Arapaho, probably near Lamar, Colorado. The more I learned, the more uneasy I felt.

Colorado now has just one Native American reservation, the Ute Mountain Reservation in southern Colorado. The Utes enjoyed the beauty of the mountain area we live in long before we all did. As nomads, though, they didn't claim territory—they moved from place to place with the buffalo.

Our little tribes from each class formed one larger tribe from Wilmot Elementary School. We carried our tepee covers and gear up

Buffalo Park Road. The children carried backpacks and tepee poles. We walked single file in each other's tracks (as the original Native Americans did so enemy tribes would not be able to get an accurate count to prepare for attack).

Our usual feelings of competition and individuality seemed to disappear as we tried to emulate the group consciousness of the tribe. Evidently, the Indians did not approve of competition, and some Indians refused to take government land allotments as individuals because they wanted to keep group loyalty. What a contrast to our own cultural aspirations: the latest toys (for kids and adults), bigger houses, more acreage than the neighbors.

After the opening ceremony, our tribe set up our teepees. The children were involved in the setup and felt proud of the results. They seemed more eager to help than usual. One of the other mom volunteers said Native American children were quiet and babies were carried on cradle boards and taught not to cry so the enemy wouldn't hear them.

Sitting in a circle next to our tepee, we dined on beef jerky, seeds, and homemade corn bread. Our activities included tracking animals, feeling things while blindfolded—such as a pine cone, a large boulder, and a well-worn path—and playing a game called "Throw an Arrow Through a Rolling Wheel." The wheel was constructed out of a hula hoop and string. The activity called "Too Many People" took us to an illegal fireplace full of cans and broken glass. We discussed how people can ruin the land and how illegal campfires could burn down all the trees, plants, and animals in open space parks.

"The Medicine Wheel" was our last activity before taking down the tepee. We each put smooth stones into a circle of dirt with spokes. Each stone represented such things as stars, the sky, the rainbow, snow, lakes, birds, animals, and people. The wheel represented the circle of life and related elements.

As we took down the tepee, we felt an unmistakable kinship with each other and a fondness for the aspen-studded land where we had camped.

Other feelings, deeper and perhaps stronger, ran through me as well: loss and regret.

The Canyon Courier, November 7, 1990 (revised)

24

Defining Roles for Women

Sometimes it's confusing. What do I tell my daughter about the changing roles of women? I'm different from my mother, and my daughter is already different from me.

When I say my mother and I are different in our roles, let me give you an example. Like other mothers who stayed home with their kids on the block, my mother took care of my brother and me full-time and accepted that my father, after working all week, would play golf on the weekend. She never asked him to babysit so that she could go out and have "fun" herself.

So when she found out that I was planning a weekend retreat and leaving the kids with my husband, she made a remark, "Oh, isn't he wonderful to take care of the kids?"

"Mom, my husband encourages me to take a weekend because he does the same thing himself," I say. "He also helps with the kids when I am working freelance." Mom pondered this. Most husbands didn't stay home with the kids while the wives worked or had "fun." But then the fathers weren't as close to their kids as many fathers in my generation.

Times have changed.

A flyer came home from my children's elementary school titled "50 Tips for Raising Kids." First tip: Avoid gender bias. That is a good concept but hard to achieve. The American Association of University Women did studies revealing that teachers do not call on girls as much as the boys in school, which lowers the girls' self-esteem.

I did a double take when I read it because when I taught a fourth-grade class at church, a woman observing pointed out to me that I called on two aggressive boys frequently and ignored the well-behaved girls. I didn't realize I was doing it.

So what do I tell my daughter? To be more aggressive in school? Certainly I want her to get as good an education as the boys, and I don't want her self-esteem to be lowered by being ignored. But how does a loud, aggressive girl get ahead in school and business and at the same time make friends?

It's all such a balancing act—how to be a woman, mother, employee, boss, etc., in this world. My daughter asked me out of the blue, "Mom, why don't you have a career?"

"Whoa," I said, taken aback. "I guess you don't remember me going to work as an ESL teacher."

"Oh."

But my daughter's question stuck with me like a thorn in my side. She didn't see that raising children is an investment in their future, a career choice.

And what about her? Did I want her to have a career? Yes, most definitely. Most women have to help support their families or at least themselves. And working can bring great satisfaction in life.

My daughter is intelligent and creative, and likely will have some challenging job opportunities. On the flip side I hope she will also make family a priority if she gets married. How will she balance all these things?

Probably she will do it differently than my mother did it, and in a different way from the way I'm doing it. But I'm sure one thing will be the same if she has a family after she graduates from college.

She will have to develop the ability to handle many important things in one day. Hopefully I'll see her do awesome things. Go for it, kid.

The Canyon Courier, September 29, 1993

25

It's Christmas Time

I know it's December because I am shopping all the time. I even shop in my sleep. Last night, when I woke up at 3 a.m., I was dreaming about purchasing a plant at K-Mart.

My friend Gayle tells me she finished all her shopping for gifts before Thanksgiving so that she could enjoy December.

Wow.

Every day, as I prepare for Christmas—shopping, wrapping presents, getting them ready to mail, writing cards, baking cookies, decorating the tree, and running back to the store for more gifts or making last-minute presents, I think of Gayle and how smart she is.

I know I have gone over the edge when I find myself eating a TV dinner while driving a car. Yes, I am consuming a sweet-and-sour chicken meal with a fork while driving. It is doubly dangerous because I wear a light gold silk blouse under a wool blazer. Next to me, my dinner rides shotgun.

I attempt to figure out how to replace my nephew's gift, which I bought thirty miles away from my home in the wrong size. But drive all that distance?

As I stop at the red light near my house, I feel hunger pangs. Slyly I pick up the fork and stick it into a small chunk of chicken. I glance around to see if anyone watches me. Ever so slowly I sneak a bite. It tastes even better than food at a picnic.

The light turns green. I set the fork down and step on the gas. I wonder if I have gone nuts eating a TV dinner while driving down the road. And I'm the woman who supposedly never serves TV dinners to my family, according to a newspaper article written about me. (I said that to the reporter and meant it—at the time.)

But the chicken tastes good. With my hands on the steering wheel I glance at the road, study the traffic, and then slowly remove my right hand from the wheel and put a forkful of rice and chicken in my mouth.

This procedure has a rhythm to it. Put the fork into the food, drive, look at the road, look at the food, look at the road, look at the food, look at the road, look at the food, and then move fork into mouth smoothly. Even though it flies against everything I've ever believed about how one should eat dinner, I feel like a ballerina. I can do two things at once magnificently. Not a single grain of rice falls on my blouse. I pass Main Street and head out of Evergreen.

A police officer sees me and pulls me over with his flashing red lights.

"Ma'am, it is dangerous to eat and drive," he says.

"But it's a Healthy Choice dinner."

His eyes twinkle. He suppresses a laugh. "Ma'am, but distraction while operating a vehicle is hazardous."

"Sorry officer, the holiday stress ..."

He studies me. "I'll give you a warning. Eat before you drive, or pull over and park if you must eat."

"I promise you, officer, never again." I mean it and do not attempt to eat a TV dinner while driving again. It's the type of thing you only do once in your life. It's something you do if it's December and you're a working mother and you don't get prepared early for the Christmas crush. For my well-prepared friend Gayle, December and Christmas are fun. For me, since becoming a mother of two, Christmas is a scattershot rush to the finish line.

The Canyon Courier, December 1993

26

Why Shouldn't "Older" Women Have Babies?

Since 1975 the rate of first babies being born to women aged thirty to thirty-five has doubled in the United States. It is a noticeable trend, especially among college women, but in this case was it the Christmas spirit?

In December, a fifty-nine-year-old London woman gave birth to twins on purpose. She had the fertilized eggs artificially implanted into her in a fertility clinic in Rome. It's a good thing she married a younger man, forty-five, or they would both run out of breath. But at forty-five, will even he be bouncing out of bed to feed the babies?

"That woman is a lunatic. She needs a psychiatrist," a friend comments.

"Why would she want to be pregnant at that age?" another friend asks. Four of us women whose children go to the same school drink coffee together. We consider ourselves older moms because we didn't start until our thirties having babies and now have kids who are at least twelve years old.

But the mother of twins from London could put us into an identity crisis—she's almost sixty and starting a new family. Time will tell whether the woman and her husband in London made a wise choice. They have only just begun. I'll wait to interview them until they've driven to at least fifty children's soccer games.

But back to reality with this group of moms who have been in the trenches a while. After visiting over coffee, I see threads of common feelings.

In our twenties none of us wanted kids. We weren't interested in children back then because we all had a life with fulfilling work. One friend says, "In the early days of our marriage we called it 'child free.'"

Another thing we have in common is that we all went to college and married around thirty. Our biological clocks changed our attitudes about having children. In the twenties we knew we still had time.

We agree the downside of being an older mom is the lack of energy. "I'm forty-four—I don't think I can do sitting on Santa's lap one more time," one mother says.

Another factor that affects mothers starting their families late in life is their aging parents. Older moms often find themselves in a crunch with caring for children and parents at the same time. I myself feel that crunch.

One friend spent a quarter of last year driving to another state to take care of her mother. But the good thing about it was that her children learned to be sensitive to older people, learned to take blood pressure readings, and learned to be aware of signals that Grandma needed something.

Other comments from older moms were:

"It takes longer to recover from childbirth. Those twenty-year-old moms pop the kid and are back in tight jeans the next day."

"As a mom in my forties, it's easier to separate the wheat from the chaff."

"There's less pressure to succeed—people think you're a lost cause."

"There's less desire for materialistic things. I had a sports car in my twenties. I don't need one now, so I can buy things for my kids."

"I don't envy anyone."

"When I thought of having a baby, I forgot to add twenty years."

We are a noisy, laughing group, the four of us drinking coffee and eating breakfast at the local café. There is one last comment, my favorite:

"These younger moms have trouble with their adult kids moving back in with them. When mine wants to move back, I'll be dead."

The Canyon Courier, January 1994

27

The Wild West Is Still Alive in Yellowstone

"It will be a piece of cake," Gayle Brumelle assured my husband, Mike, and me regarding a snowmobiling adventure in Yellowstone National Park over New Years. "You can bring the kids."

We prepared for the trip, packing face masks, caps, long underwear, heavy pants, coats, socks, and boots for the four of us.

I knew it would be cold in late December, but not having a crystal ball, I couldn't imagine how cold.

At the beginning, the tour company drops our gang of twenty off with two guides, snowmobiles, and belongings at the south end of Yellowstone. We bungee cord our packs to the backs of the snowmobiles, which resemble motorcycles on skis.

After a two-minute lesson on how to control the heavy machines, brake lever on the left, gas lever on the right, we hear "Mount 'em up!" Dressed in black, our gang becomes the Arctic Hells Angels.

Engines wail in the frosty air.

Following our leader, we kick our snowmobiles up to 40 mph. Son Jim, age six, rides on the back of his father's machine and daughter Lily, age nine, has her arms around my waist on the back of mine. My snowmobile fishtails and swings from side to side on the ice. I grip the handles and fear we might go into a skid.

"It's OK, just detach your shoulders from the bottom of your body!" hollers our guide.

"A piece of cake—my ass," I mumble.

The geyser at Old Faithful sets to go off and we arrive barely in time to admire the gushing natural phenomenon.

Adventure usually requires going beyond one's limits, and this trip qualifies. The first night in Yellowstone, the thermometer on our cabin plunges to forty degrees below zero. The next day it is so chilly along the road that I wonder if we will survive the trip. A particular challenge for me is the sheet ice on the floor of the outhouse.

After we've been on the road a few hours, Lily asks me, "What are those white spots on your cheeks, Mom?"

"Frostbite," someone else says.

Alarmed, I rub my cheeks with my gloves. The spots eventually disappear. After riding eighty miles to the northern boundary of Yellowstone, we huddle together and thaw out at the hotel in Gardiner, Montana. I wonder if the frostbite has damaged my brain and I have mistakenly joined a radical snowmobiling cult. We stay at Buffalo Bill Cody's hunting lodge on the eastern boundary of Yellowstone, a place so historically preserved that I sniff the spirit of Buffalo Bill present in the dining room. Given my experience with rodeos, horses, and cowboys, I feel right at home.

Wild animals rule Yellowstone. Bald eagles perch together on a branch near the lodge. Coyotes, bighorn sheep, and elk own the woods.

On the last day a herd of buffalo blocks our path. Here we are: twenty freezing humans on our ridiculous snowmobiles in a confrontation with forty thousand pounds of potential damage.

We wear three layers of socks, boots, long underwear, quilted snowmobiling suits, goggles, helmets, and bandannas while the buffalo stand in the road with nothing on but their curly fur coats. The formidable herd spreads across the road staring at our pack of intruders. We blow steam at each other out of our respective nostrils.

Awed by the confrontation, I try not to show fear, but if the buffalo charge us I'll pee in my pants.

Our guide, Tom, waves his arms and shouts at the buffalo, "Move on. Get out! Get out, you hear me?"

The gigantic horned animals pay as little attention to Tom as they would to Tweetie Bird. They don't care how much technology we represent. They have the power.

With our butts turning to ice, we wait for an hour before the buffalo casually amble on. It is the Chinese year of the boar, but it should have been called "the year of the buffalo."

Yellowstone on snowmobiles—what a great adventure. Only one woman had an accident. She broke her arm when she squeezed the gas lever instead of the brake lever and sailed off an embankment.

After returning the snowmobiles, outer gear, and helmets, I reluctantly said good-bye to our friends, and with my family headed for our Ford Ranger pickup truck. The process of parting reminded me of working on a movie shoot, where a community works together with a purpose, then when it's all over every one goes their separate ways. Back in Colorado we return to the rat race and stress of metropolitan life. I feel nostalgic for the arctic rides and shared adventures with our pack of humans.

But I don't wail because I know more adventures lie ahead.

The Canyon Courier, January, 1991

Freezing our butts off in Yellowstone National Park

28

Climbing Fools

Was it a streak of madness? During the July heat wave of one-hundred-degree days, when any sane person would sip iced tea in an air-conditioned room, my husband, Mike, and our son, Jim, thirteen, planned to climb Mount of the Holy Cross, which has a reputation for endangering the lives of many hikers. The 14,005-foot peak in Colorado is named for the snow cross that forms on the face.

Because of the blistering heat, I declined the invitation to join them, but the morning they prepared to leave, I had a change of heart, packed up my gear, and hopped in the Ford pickup with them.

I hadn't reached the summit of a 14,000-foot peak in seven years but figured I could climb it because I'd been exercising regularly.

When we begin the hike at the trailhead at 7 a.m., it's already hot and the sky is empty of clouds and quiet as a coiled snake.

We plaster on sunscreen and adjust our hats. Wearing backpacks we commence the five-mile trek to the top. After about three miles of trudging up and down the trail, I catch a glimpse of the steep rock summit. I gasp, "We're climbing that?" I have serious concerns about the size of this mountain.

As we hike above timberline, the trail disappears in a field of boulders. We scramble up the rocks and follow "cairns" (tall piles of stones hikers create to mark trails). I think we're keeping a good pace, but soon a young woman, an older man, and two teenage boys pass us. They repeat the climbing wisdom that one should be off the summit of a 14,000-foot peak by noon because of the threat of lightning. They hurry along, heading for the summit.

The weather remains hot and sunny until 1 p.m., when we approach the steepest part of the climb to the summit. A dark cloud blows over the sun.

An older man hikes down toward us on his way off the top. He says, "I recommend you turn back because of the threat of lightning." I grimace.

Mike, who has already climbed the mountain with another group, is reluctant to continue. "Let's go back," he says. Jim and I keep going; we have "summit fever." In the distance, thunder rumbles. Mike climbs with us, "Better make it fast," he says. Jim takes off ahead of us and we lose sight of him.

The weather adds tension, but we climb over rocks, hoping we will find Jim. For another twenty minutes we climb up, up, and more up. With my energy maxed out, I summit the Mount of the Holy Cross. Jim is already there gazing around. "Hey, you're not supposed to leave us," I say to him. "We were worried about you." Exhausted, I collapse next to a boulder and Mike and I eat our peanut butter and jelly sandwiches. The beauty of the view is incomparable.

I glance at my watch—it is 2 p.m., a dangerous time to be on the summit. Clouds form an angry mass over our heads, and thunder claps. "Let's go," I say, realizing climbing to the top could have been a very big mistake.

The clouds close in as we begin our descent—against son Jim's protests. "Don't rush me," he says.

As we make our way down, stepping boulder to boulder, raindrops pelt us. Jim stops, as he's out of steam. We pause for him to wolf down his sandwich. Lightning sparks near us. I urge Jim to hustle. "Finish up that sandwich unless you want to be toast," I say.

Jim, who weighs 135 pounds, says to me, "Carry me, Mom."

"No!"

The rain hammers us harder until our jeans look like a rock star's shiny pants. Our hands, feet, and entire bodies are soaking wet. We have packed for a heat wave, not for the dramatic entrance of the cold, rainy monsoon season.

For three hours, wet and cold, we hustle along. The afternoon becomes darker and colder. We slide down a snowfield and lose the trail. I fear we are in serious trouble and pray hypothermia won't set in.

Possibly by the grace of a merciful God, the trail appears again. We stagger back to the car twelve hours from the time we left. I shake with relief, thankful that we found the trail back.

I believe there is a streak of insanity in anyone who climbs 14,000-foot peaks. You spend so much energy and incur risk of physical harm every time you climb one. Still, when you get back sore and exhausted, wet and cold, wanting dry clothes more than life itself, you find yourself plotting going up another one, even though you could have taken the same expenditure of energy and painted the kitchen, tiled the bathroom, and put in a toilet all in one day.

The incomparable beauty and dramatic scenery, combined with the tiny, brilliant flowers above timberline, all feel like some kind of divine love letter. You're breathing fresh air, and you experience a taste of heaven because you have entered a pristine sacred place that has the scent of God.

The Canyon Courier, September 2, 1998

Part Five

You Fall Off, You Get Back On

*Don't be afraid to cry. It will free your mind
of sorrowful thoughts.*
—Hopi proverb

My husband, Mike, and I tried for years to work things out. But during our twenty-four years of marriage we grew apart. The empty nest accentuated our problems. In 2003 the reasons to separate became crystal clear. But I hated the idea of breaking up our family.

In the sanctuary of my church I gazed at the crucifix and stained glass windows. On the kneeler I bowed my head and prayed, Please help me, God. I didn't expect to hear back words but what I heard back is: I will provide.

Was it really God talking? Did He know my situation and what was going to happen before I would? It seems that He did.

After making the drastic decision to move on, I faced the classic conundrum for a woman in my situation in her fifties. By separating, our conflicts vanished. But in their place, the big boots of loneliness entered, stomping on my heart and mind. Empty nest, empty house, empty everything.

Thankfully this period lasted only five years, during which time I became a professional on-call hospital chaplain with a pager, a name tag, and a paycheck. Just like the old days when thrown from a horse, I fell off and got on again.

29

Dance Shoes Lead to Wedding

Life often surprises me. Living single in a Colorado mountain town, I doubt I'll ever remarry. Besides the lack of available men, weddings give me the willies. But after I've been alone for a few years, my neighbor Sally invites me to take ballroom dance lessons.

When the evening arrives, I wear a straight black dress, pearls, and platinum metallic shoes. Sally wears a blue-flowered dress with a full skirt. We barely recognize each other and both look so elegant we declare we have a mutual admiration society. Sally drives me to the dance studio on the west side of Denver.

We park and as I get out of her car, I step in a hole. "Ay yi yi!" I say.

Sally grabs a roll of paper towels from her trunk and we clean off my shoe. Feeling clumsy, and wearing a scuffed shoe to my first dance, I'm on edge. At age sixty, I wonder why I'm not more poised and self-possessed.

Inside the dance hall, we pay our $10 fee. I nervously gaze at a group of women in evening dresses with twirly skirts. The men—mostly wearing suits and ties—wait across the dance floor from the women. As I catch the scent of mingled perfumes, the memory of my being a shy wallflower at junior high cotillion flashes across my mental movie screen.

"Find a partner for the waltz, and then we'll rotate," the instructor says. "Women, create a strong frame so the men can guide you. No spaghetti arms allowed!"

Being a woman some call "bossy," following the steps of a man proves challenging for me.

"Relax. Let me lead!" my dance partner says.

With fits and starts, I let go of my ringleader tendencies and begin to enjoy the waltz. Maybe I can learn ballroom dancing after all. After the class the instructor says, "Mary, those flats aren't so good, you should buy some really good dance shoes." And she tells me where to get them.

The next day on a narrow street with quaint and artsy boutiques, I can't locate the dance store. A life-size wooden cutout of a farmer standing on the porch of Grandfather's Books catches my eye. Books are displayed in the window, including a copy of *On the Road* by Jack Kerouac. Figuring a book person will have the information I need, I open the door, causing bells to jingle.

A handsome man with silver hair and glasses is eating potato chips and reading *The Hobbit*. It turns out he's the owner, Dick. I ask him for directions to the dance store.

"Dance store, yes. I know where it is, but tell me something first. Who are you?" He engages me in conversation and we talk for an hour, discovering we have much in common, such as loving books, poetry, and movies. I notice he doesn't wear a wedding ring, and I wonder if he has a girlfriend. He jokes about having fifty-two angels who got me lost and brought me in. "Do you want to be on the board of my nonprofit bookstore?" he asks.

"That's a nice offer—I'll consider it," I say smiling. And from our great conversation, I agree to help in his bookstore as a part-time volunteer. As far as dancing, he says he does do a little jitterbug.

And so with Dick's directions I arrive at the dance store and succeed in buying a pair of black Capezio dance shoes, not realizing I have just met the man who will change my life.

After volunteering in Dick's bookstore and many get-togethers, I wonder if we should keep it the way it is—a friendship. A year later something romantic happens. After attending a centering prayer group on Valentine's Day, we go Dutch to a romantic Italian restaurant!

It's Valentine's Day and cupid has shot us with his arrows. Our relationship steps up to another level. After more outings, movies, dancing, and dinners (and some aren't even Dutch), we find we are together more than apart. At a mountain lake near my home, Dick gets down on bended knee, and since he is so much taller than me, it is a touching sight to look down at him and see him gazing up into my eyes.

"Will you marry me?" he asks.

I feel thrilled at his offer but also hesitant at potential complications.

When I visit my ninety-year-old mother, who lives in a nursing home, I say, "Dick has asked me to marry him."

"What are you waiting for?" she asks.

"I'm waiting to make up my mind," I say.

Luckily Dick keeps his offer of marriage open. He jokes that he won't marry me unless I bring my tabby cat. "She's the dowry," he says. His sense of humor entices me, and we continue to see each other. "I know you're in love with me, I can see it in your eyes," he says.

"I can see it in your eyes, too," I say.

I finally make up my mind and say to Dick, "Yes, I'll marry you. How about a destination wedding in Mexico?"

"Oh no," Dick says. "I want my friends to come to the wedding. They won't be able to make it to Mexico, especially my friend with MS in a wheelchair."

I can't argue. "I concede," I say. "My mother's in a wheelchair, too. Now both she and your friend will be able to attend."

Then it's time to announce the big news of our impending wedding to friends and relatives.

When I tell Sally I'm getting married, she says, "Really? You?"

"Yes, me."

"What are you going to wear?" she asks.

"I don't know about the dress but for good luck I'll wear the dance shoes I bought the day I met Dick."

"Good idea."

A few days later my childhood friend Claudia helps me shop for a bridal dress. But with my light skin in November, with a white or off-white dress, instead of a bride I look like a visiting spirit. With my friend's collaboration, I choose a white lacy top with a long black shimmering skirt. The outfit looks lovely with my black Capezio ankle-strap dance shoes.

Because my mother is in fragile health, we hold the ceremony in the guest dining room of her nursing home. The day of the wedding, when I walk in, Dick is waiting for me. He looks handsome in his new wool blazer, slacks, and shined shoes. Dick's blue eyes light up as we approach each other. My mother and elderly aunt beam. I am thrilled to feel love for Dick and his love for me as we're surrounded by the warmth of family and friends. With a priest-chaplain friend officiating, Dick and I say our sacred vows to each other, promising to share our hopes, dreams, fears, and laughter.

And after three years am I ever glad I married him—the companionship, conversation, and physical affection are all delightful. To love and be loved again, I never thought it would happen.

And I have a fun dance partner who smiles at me on the dance floor and still calls me his "beautiful bride."

Sometimes I wonder about Dick's fifty-two angels. Did they put us together?

Yes, life is full of surprises.

Colorado Community Media newspapers, June 9, 2011

Dick's and my wedding, 2009

30

Let's Look at Each Other

What we see of people at work and family members at home is heads bent over cell phones or computers. We see people's backs and profiles working over tasks or playing games online. Since most of the eye contact with other humans on the planet has disappeared, there's no reason for women to put on makeup or for men to shave. The back of our heads is all that counts. Don't worry about bangs for women or receding hairlines for men. Few people will ever see that part of us.

Today I visit a new doctor. Typing into a small laptop, he enters the room backwards, giving me a good look at his posterior. I cannot tell you what color his eyes are because I never see them during the visit. I feel distant and annoyed. My regular physician for ten years has gone to locking her face into her laptop screen during our visits. I don't see her eyes nor does she see mine anymore. I could wear a patch over my eye, and she wouldn't notice. Luckily I have found a new doctor who listens and doesn't carry a computer. I believe healing of patients comes from doctors looking at their patients and listening.

A friend of mine says, "My son is on his iPhone so much that I never see his eyes. We were playing ping-pong and he had the paddle in one hand and the cell phone in the other! He was texting while he was playing!"

"What kind of father-son-bonding is that?" I gasp.

"Not much."

"So who won the game?"

"He did!"

"While texting? That adds insult to injury."

He laughs. "At least I thought while he was texting, I could beat him."

"Darn right!" I say. Another friend of mine, who is a hospital administrator, tells me, "I text my coworker in the office next door."

"Why? Does he have a contagious disease?"

"Not that I know of."

"Then why doesn't one of you get up and walk into the other's office?"

"Texting is easier. It's more sanitary."

Something's wrong here. Do we have to go to movies to see people's eyes? Think of Billy Crystal, Meryl Streep, or George Clooney. What do you think of first? For me, I think of their eyes. They have become rich and famous giving us eye contact through a movie screen.

Even before all the current technology emerged like an army from a Trojan horse, people struggled with eye contact. One famous scene in the movie *Citizen Kane* shows Kane (Orson Welles) and his wife in a collage of scenes at the breakfast table. The first scene starts out romantic, where they look into each other's eyes, then whirls forward through time, and finally degenerates to the last scene where at breakfast Kane totally blocks out his wife with the newspaper. There is more than one way to avoid connectedness.

I'm not innocent here. Just the other day, my husband, Dick, and I realized we hadn't looked at each other for two days. We had been at home reading, staring into our laptops and writing—a real marathon. Dick would grunt out comments like, "You've got to read this, honey."

"Sure, just let me just finish this."

"Yeah, good." He continues to read the funny papers.

"Could you look at me?" I say.

"What do you mean, look at you?"

"You know, with your eyes."

He glances up for a second and blinks.

"I'm your wife. Remember me?"

"Aren't you the barrel racer?"

"Yeah, and you're the sugar beet farmer," I say. "I like seeing your eyes."

"I like seeing yours, too. They're beautiful."

Yes, something magical happens when we connect eye to eye. It helps us network, land jobs, make friends, and fall in love.

Colorado Community Media newspapers, February 2012

31

How to File Your Papers

Ha, ha—this is a joke, me writing about filing. I'm only choosing this topic because maybe if I have to write about it, I'll learn to do it.

My current filing system: In the night, ideas for columns, poems, or books pop into my brain. My filing practice for these moments: I keep 3 × 5 recipe cards and a pen on my bedside table. A flashlight is helpful. Once the ideas are jotted down, I must stash these tidbits in a place I can retrieve them in the next century. This way of herding cards like cattle all over the house works for me and might work for you.

Hide your ideas in drawers, bathrobe pockets, and the blender. The main thing is they are SAFE.

A tip for you regarding bigger projects than ideas in the night: Tape the scribbled pages of the great American novel you're working on to your walls so you can view the whole story at once. You start in the bathroom and continue out into the hall. In the kitchen, paste and tape the pages on the outside of cupboards, walls, and the refrigerator.

The pages of your bestseller when pasted up create an arch on the walls around the dining room. Don't let anyone tell you that you don't have a story arc.

Extra tip: I do not encourage you to attach pages of your book to the outside of your house. I tried this once and the wind came up and blew part of my story into the neighbor's yard. He quickly published a similar novel to mine before I could say "Bingo."

I confess this tendency of mine to tape my novel on the walls of my house may explain why only the shorter pieces ever see the light of day. My blockbuster novel decorating my walls looks so nice there, especially when the alternative means taking the time to actually decipher my handwriting and type it all. Maybe next week, or some other month.

If you would like to read my novel, you'd better hotfoot it over to my house fast. The painters are coming.

Colorado Community Media newspapers, June 2013

32

My Husband Refuses to Multitask at 70 mph

My husband does not like to have a deep emotional conversation with me sitting next to him while he's driving 70 mph. Now me, I can discuss anything while driving 70 mph on a freeway, on the open road, with the person riding shotgun. I'm a woman, and my growing talent at multitasking began when I discovered I could clean up the kitchen, talk to my neighbor on the phone, and country western line dance all while my infant daughter sat in a backpack tugging on my hair.

They say men accomplish more in the business world than mothers at home because they compartmentalize their work, focusing on one thing at a time. Michelangelo couldn't have multitasked while he was painting the ceiling of the Sistine Chapel. The results of his one-track-mind work are admired by a gazillion tourists each year at the Vatican.

The multitasking we all know about—driving while talking on the cell phone—is dangerous because when the driver needs to react quickly to something on the road, she is still engaged mentally with the conversation in another location. This has certainly proven true for me.

I've discovered I'm so much happier when away from home on vacation, staying out of the car, shutting off the phone and computers, and doing just one thing at a time. Since I can't afford to be on vacation all the time, maybe I should join a primitive tribe of humans who have the common sense to do one thing at a time such as weaving, playing the flute, or shucking corn.

I have a sneaking suspicion that the primitive tribes have better social interaction, better focus, and a better sense of presence than we do, or at least than I do.

I am humbled by this thought.

Colorado Community Media newspapers, September 2011

33

Bombing My Way Through a Comedy Routine

Back in my twenties, I performed comedy routines at the Comedy Store and Improvisation Nightclub in Hollywood. Bud Friedman, the owner of the Improv and Starmaker, encouraged me: "You are the female Will Rogers, with a little more practice I suggest you audition for the TV show *Laugh-In*." I felt pretty optimistic about standup, although admittedly my audience didn't always respond as positively as Bud did. In any case, the demands of my first baby sidelined me.

Not too long ago, though, I caught the comedy bug again and began to perform routines for the Robert Benchley Society Awards Dinner, senior centers, and birthday parties.

My childhood friend Claudia calls me. "Mary, I need help with a dinner I'm putting on for the residents in my adult condo complex."

"What do you need?" I ask.

"Do you think you could do a comedy routine for the dinner?" she asks.

"Yikes. How many people are you expecting?"

"Around seventy-five."

My throat tightens. No way for me to make eye contact or connect with that many people. *But this could be my early break into over-sixty-age stardom. Maybe I'll get discovered by a retired producer or club owner with great connections. I'll perform again on classy stages in upscale clubs. Joan Rivers—are you quaking in your sequined high heels up there in Heaven?*

"I'll need a microphone," I say.

"No problem."

I'll also need a routine, I think but don't say. I realize my big talk about my little experience may just have set me up for a bit of a disaster. And not, I also realize, for the first time.

Even though I break out in a rash from nervousness, I work up a routine. I think about my Comedy Store standup—maybe I can use some of that material. It crosses my mind that my audience is quite different, and I'm quite different, more "mature," to put it kindly. But I let the thought run right across my mind and out the other side. The night of the party, to my horror I discover I will go on first, at 5 p.m., before the people have had drinks or food.

Queasiness overwhelms me. The fancy room is brightly lit and full of dressed-up adults at the worst part of their day, waiting for food.

I discover I'm an added act. The crowd expects a British female singing trio after dinner, and nothing between their arrival and getting fed. I test the microphone—the people at the front table look askance at me. Do they think I'm a stranger who just wandered in uninvited? Am I?

When I pop out my first few jokes, they laugh weakly. Then they start pounding their silverware. "We want food."

"How long are you going to be up there?" a man catcalls.

I'm now angry as well as humiliated. I shout back: "I'll be up here all night and I already ate all the food!" Someone laughs.

My knees wobble and my jaw feels stiff. Then I say, "The world has changed for me. Twenty years ago pot was illegal and you could smoke cigarettes. Now pot is legal and you can't smoke anywhere." When they stare at me coldly, I say, "I'm a Pisces working for scale. I'm just floundering around."

"I'll take a flounder dinner!" a man quips.

At the end of my routine, I say ridiculously, "You've been a great audience." They laugh at that because it's a lie.

I feel alarmed, embarrassed, and murderous. I want to strangle my friend.

Of course, when the dust settled I came to terms with the truth: I flopped and floundered without anybody's help. And there was a little something, that big awkward laugh at the end, maybe, that lit another little spark.

What if I took material from my life now? Hmmm.

Not too long after this debacle, I pulled my performing self together. My new routine includes this story, and, lo and behold, people usually laugh right with me:

I see my plastic surgeon about removing a lump from my eyelid. The plastic surgeon studies my eyelid under a bright light and says, "You need your eyelids lifted. We'll take care of your lump while we do it."

Vaguely interested in vanity surgery, I ask, "How much is that?"

"$3,500."

I gasp.

"But if we just do your eyes, you'll have young eyes and old cheeks," he says. "We should do an entire face lift."

Taken aback, I ask, "How much would that cost?"

"Face lift: $10,000. All together eyes and face: $13,500."

I collapse back in my chair. "For removing that tiny lump? If I wanted a con job I'd go down to the local prison."

Ba-boom chick!

Colorado Community Media newspapers, April 2013

Bombing as a comedienne, 2012

34

Men and Women See Things Differently

Do men and women ever truly communicate? It's an age-old question bandied about over the ages by bards such as William Shakespeare and Mel Gibson.

My friend Judy and I are having breakfast. "Men have ruled the world as a species," she says. "When they are with their wives, they are not where they are. When my husband and I are getting ready to go somewhere, I look at my watch, see that we might be late, and say to him, 'Would you stop planning your next woodworking project and take a shower?'"

I laugh. "Dick is often the same way," I say. "He has so many projects on his mind, such as writing poetry, building tables, and pitching his next softball game, that he's distracted."

"You're right," she says. "Your husband is the same way."

"A year ago when I broke my foot and couldn't put weight on it, Dick was pushing me in a wheelchair at the mall," I say. "A bookstore attracted him and he dashed off, leaving me alone in the wheelchair in the middle of the mall walkway. I felt like strangling him."

"I'll bet you did," Judy says. "My mate of forty years pulls up at church to let me out with the car running and doesn't put on the brake. If his mind wanders, he could forget I'm getting out and I could get injured. I talked to him about it and he said he'd work on it."

"Men and women think so differently, it's a challenge to live together," I say. "Even if they have a great career, most women instinctively pay attention to people."

"And some men's minds are preoccupied with planning and conquering things," she says.

"Yes," I say. "When Dick gets that faraway look in his eyes, he's daydreaming he's by himself trampling our opponents in the Super Bowl and later conquering Newfoundland."

"Ha! He sounds like Walter Mitty."

For me to understand how Dick thinks, or any man thinks, sometimes I purposely sit in the men's corner at big parties. A group of men at happy hour before book club talk about electrical engineering, water management, and geology. I sit riveted, not saying a word. I feel energized. *Aha, this is how men think! I've discovered the secret of the universe.*

Now if I can just get quickie degrees in electrical engineering, flood management and geological rock throwing, maybe I'll be able to communicate with Dick. And, possibly, while we're shopping he won't leave the building.

Colorado Community Media newspapers, April 2012

35

Helping the Homeless Women

You rocked the earth, split it open:
Repair the cracks for it totters.
You made your people go through hardship.
—Psalm 60:4-6

We place bottom sheets on cots. Then we add top sheets, quilts, and stuff pillows into pillowcases because twenty homeless women will soon be arriving for dinner, fellowship, and bed. This event, put on by a motley group of volunteers, happens every Wednesday night in a church basement in Denver.

I go to help, to give back, to do service.

Today the women file in and sign their names on a form held to a clipboard. It strikes me that I somehow expect them to look different from me or the people I know, but they don't. Some have bright eyes, shiny faces, and clean hair. Others look tired with hair hidden beneath caps or scarves. Any one of them could be me, depending on the day and my state of mind. I have worn an aqua-colored beaded necklace with three strands today, so they will see something beautiful. A woman says, "I like your necklace."

We feed them black beans with rice in a sauce, cornbread, brownies, and iced tea, and I help clear the dishes from the tables when they are through.

"Can I have seconds?" a hungry woman asks. I'm told to inform her to wait until all twenty are fed.

"Put your backpacks on a cot so others will know it's taken," the volunteer leader announces. They do so and a homeless woman says she wants to smoke. Someone must go with them, so I take a group of smokers outside. Several women say they are married or engaged. One woman says, "There are no shelters for married couples. My husband is in a men's shelter." I feel grateful that I am not separated from my husband every night like some of the homeless women are from their husbands.

We are on the sidewalk by a bench outside the church and it is a perfect night weather-wise. Several sit and the rest of us stand forming a circle. We could be a gang—there are enough of us.

A fiftyish woman tells me, "We ended up homeless—that is, my husband and me—when the bank foreclosed on us and kicked us off our land in Montana."

The thought of losing property, especially my home, frightens me. I think of the millions of homeless refugees overseas: Iraqis, Egyptians, Syrians, Sudanese ...

After dinner is finished for both sets of women I offer to help prepare breakfast for the next morning. It will be a frittata with cut-up bread, eggs, milk, and chilies.

The woman in charge asks, "Mary, can you cut up the red and green chilies?"

"Sure," I say, not knowing what I'm getting into. After washing and seeding the little wretches, my eyes water. Chile juice flows over the edge of the cutting board and makes a mess. The aroma makes me cough. Everyone in the kitchen begins to gag and cough.

I continue to chop until the job is done. After I crack open thirty-six eggs and drop them into a bowl, I add milk and stir it all together. The woman in charge has placed the chopped bread and chilies and cheese into the pans. I pour the egg concoction over the top and she places the frittatas in the church refrigerator.

"Thanks, Mary, for your help."

I nod and leave.

At home I remove my aqua necklace and contact lenses. My eyes burn like never before. The vapor from the chilies must have accumulated in my eyes and under my lenses. For few moments I can't see.

The discomfort in my eyes reminds me of the women sleeping on the cots in the church basement. I get a hint of the distress they must feel.

Colorado Community Media newspapers, September 2012

36

Afghanistan Hits Home

August 18, 2009

A t my apartment in Golden, the phone rings at 8 p.m. The bad news explodes and shoots straight to my heart.

I burst into tears.

My nephew, Eden Pearl, a Special Forces Marine in Afghanistan, has been hit by a roadside bomb, what they call an IED.

"He has third-degree burns over eighty-five percent of his body," his mother, my sister-in-law, tells me.

He is her only child.

"If I lose him, I don't know what I'll do."

At this point he is in Germany and she doesn't know if he'll live through the night.

"I'm so sorry," I say, feeling devastated and helpless, but closer to her than ever.

I saw a lot of my nephew when he was younger, playing with my son on various family trips. Red hair, freckles, mischievous, and vibrantly alive.

Now he is married with a small daughter.

How could this horrible news be true? But in my gut, immediately I know it is true. Maybe because he is a Marine walking the thin line between life and death every time he steps into the Middle East.

In the newspaper and on TV, we all see the photos of young strong men and women who have died in battle. Their faces are buried at different levels of our consciousness.

But we don't usually know them personally. I didn't take them on an airplane like I did my nephew when he was two.

I have lots of photos of Eden with my kids, some of him hamming it up.

Beginning with Iraq, he had done three tours with the Marines in the Middle East.

But now the war has come home.

The effects of war have shadowed me all my life. My father had lingering effects of prison camp during World War II. My brother, a navy flight commander in Vietnam, came back with permanent disabilities.

My nephew is still asleep in a hospital in Texas that specializes in burn patients. His mother, a widow, says the people are wonderful at taking care of her son. People are praying for him. I put a prayer request with his photo as a child into several churches and his mother has done the same.

She is not a religious person but believes that prayers are helping. Everyday she's at the hospital.

Waiting.

What miracles can happen?

How will he react when he wakes up and finds out he's been disfigured, permanently disabled, and in pain?

Will he be able to find a purpose in helping other Marines who have been injured?

I doubt he can ever return to the battlefield of what we call war.

But there are other battlefields.

Hope is what is needed.

I pray if he wakes up he will see the love in his relatives' faces.

The caring in the nurses', doctors', and fellow Marines' faces.

The Marine who was with him when the bomb exploded brings Eden's dog tags and wedding ring to the hospital.

We hang onto a thin ray of hope.

Sometimes that's all we have.

The Denver Post, Your Hub, October 2009

37

Sharing a Kitchen with Watermelon Man

They say you don't really know someone until you have shared a kitchen. I hesitate to reveal what embarrassing thing my husband, Dick, who I call Watermelon Man, has learned about me since we got married. But confession is good for the soul, so promise you won't tell anyone, OK? He'd say, "My bride scatters dishes everywhere."

But my dear husband brought to our marriage his own unexpected foibles. Before we got married my mate hadn't revealed that he could eat a two-pound slice of watermelon for dinner and call it a meal. "I'll just have watermelon tonight, honey," he says.

Now he has started eating watermelon for breakfast, lunch, and dinner.

Moreover, the watermelons my groom buys are so gargantuan they look like powerful spirits from the dark side. Sometimes I suspect they rule the house.

Watermelon now takes up a full shelf in our refrigerator. The "spare watermelon" (yes, spare watermelon) is stored on the floor of the breakfast nook, where I often stumble over it and yelp so loud the cats run out of the room.

Watermelon Man stores his "second spare watermelon" (you read it right—*his second spare watermelon*) on the floor of the garage. When I get out of my car I stub my toe on the speckled green invader. "This is going too far!" I say.

Storage is just the beginning. There is also … the eating. When my hubby gets a gigantic piece of watermelon ready to eat, the juice drips off the edge of the plate and onto the hardwood floor. When I walk into the kitchen, the soles of my shoes stick to the floor with each step— snap, click, snap, click, snap.

Dealing with it means I either throw meatballs at Watermelon Man or get down and wipe the sticky mess up myself. (There's no point in asking him to wipe up, because he's a 6'2" farmer and claims he can't see that far down.)

If guests ring the doorbell—yikes. I panic. I can't bring them into the kitchen or we'll all be stuck for the evening.

His two other favorite treats besides watermelons are fresh strawberries and strawberry jelly. When he drops something red and fruity on the floor and then steps on it, I can't identify what's stuck to the hardwood. A chunk of watermelon? A squashed strawberry? A glob of jelly? Or all three? And is it a coincidence that he only wears red shirts?

Ah, well, if he can accept my dishes I suppose I can live with the melons. It could have been worse. It could have been baked beans.

Colorado Community Media newspapers, October 2011

38

The Rotating Dog

Who wants a dog 24/7? I don't. Owning a dog is just too time-consuming. I'm not alone. Doggy daycare centers have sprung up for dog owners who have careers and cannot be home to walk Fido. Jet-setting couples and singles who own dogs have to make arrangements for their beloved pooches each time they travel. It's worse than leaving a baby behind.

My solution is the rotating dog. I learned about this method of dog ownership from personal experience. My ex-husband and I managed to keep our Chihuahua, Gizmo, in the family by moving him around from home to home.

You see, Gizmo had been the family dog and then the kids went off to college. After my husband and I split up, Gizmo lived with me for a year and even spent nights at St. Joseph's Hospital when I was working twenty-four-hour shifts as an on-call chaplain. But when that got to be too much, Gizmo went to my ex's house for a year. Then he took Gizmo down to our daughter's home in New Mexico. It worked out fine for a while, but the little rascal peed on the rugs and got bounced. Gizmo moved back in with me, then the ex again, and so it went.

Evidently other dog owners have similar experiences. Our current neighbors have their daughter's dog and say the dog doesn't know where home is.

Evidence shows the nuclear family is waning and so is the nuclear dog. Dogs must be flexible if they are to survive in the current culture. It's not "Lassie Come Home" but "Lassie Rotate."

What are dogs for anyway? My mother used to say dogs get away with mischief because they wag their tails. It's fun to play Frisbee with a dog or fetch the ball. And I enjoy walking a dog if it's trained. But at home, issues arise like codependency between dogs if there are two. One dog can't be walked alone without a whine-fest by the other. And in the yard—who cleans up the poop?

So what is the answer to dog ownership these days? The answer my friend is blowing in the wind: home-hopping for dogs.

When I remember all the rotating houses with Gizmo, I feel dizzy. Gizmo's gone from this world now, and I'm remarried and have a new life. Now that I've said all this, I do miss having a doggy with a warm little face gazing at me with loving eyes.

But right now I have one little grandchild to love and adore, which seems more important than owning and caring for a dog.

If you sense my ambivalence, you're right. The thought of having a doggy companion still has a paw grip on my heart and won't let go.

Colorado Community Media newspapers, July 2012

39

Encounter with a Seagull

On a crisp Sunday morning, I am alone on the pier at Hermosa Beach, California. The ocean rocks with whitecaps, the breeze messes up my hair, and I feel invigorated. I inhale the scent of fish, and for a minute or two I imagine myself to be a mermaid with long seaweed hair.

Then knocked out of my reverie, I spot a lone surfer in a black wet suit attempting to stand up on his surfboard. A wave topples him, and he is dumped back into the sea.

On the wood railing of the pier, a seagull stands proudly and confidently. He is large, possibly eighteen inches tall, with clean gray and white feathers, yellow webbed feet, and a yellow beak. Just five feet away, he watches me with one eye.

Fascinated by his presence, I place a morsel of my protein bar in a crevice of the railing in front of him. Then I back up. The seagull inches forward, a step at a time. He zeroes in on the morsel, lifts it up in his beak, and swallows it.

"You liked the taste of that?" I ask, not expecting an answer.

"Delicious. Better than fish—not so slimy," the seagull says.

Whoa—talking seagull. Surprised, I play along. "I don't like raw fish either. I'll give you some more of my protein bar."

He pecks up each tidbit I lay on the railing.

"You're hungry," I say. "Do you mind if I ask how old you are?"

He ignores me, cleaning his feathers. Now he gazes at me with both eyes. "I've had at least seventy birthdays."

I raise my eyebrows, surprised at his verbal ability and age. "You must have seen a lot in your time here."

"I do remember the pier was built long ago. It improved my diet with the bait and scraps of fish people leave behind."

"What do you think of living in Hermosa Beach?"

"What's that?" he asks.

I wave my arm to indicate the whole area.

"Ha! You probably think I'm just a local, a townie," the seagull says. "See these wings? Sometimes I fly to the suburbs far away and hang out near the McDonald's dumpster."

Goosebumps cover my arms. I remember the time I bought Chicken McNuggets as a takeout treat for a flock of crows in Colorado. The crows were in a field near the fast-food franchise when I made my order. But when I circled around, parked my car, and rolled down my window, the crows were nowhere to be seen. A flock of seagulls swooped down around my car, which reminded me of Alfred Hitchcock's movie *The Birds*.

Oh shucks, they must be hungry, I thought. I threw the treat out my car window. Eager eaters, the seagulls flapped, squawked, and shrieked as they scarfed up the food.

"Did you ever eat Chicken McNuggets?" I ask the seagull.

"Yes, my favorite," he says.

"Were they tossed out by a lady in a white car?" I ask.

"Yes, yes. I remember it well."

"It was me."

"What a coincidence or twist of fate. I did fly out to the hinterlands a few times. But mostly I stay around here at Seagull Hangout." He flaps his wings to indicate Hermosa Beach.

"Seagull Hangout," I repeat. I consider how each animal species sees things from their own point of view.

And then I wonder if I'm being gullible.

The seagull turns, lifts off the railing, and flies away without a word.

Colorado Community Media newspapers, February 2013

Seagull, Hermosa Beach

40

A Mother Like No Other

"Your mother is a tough-as-nails cowgirl," her friend Alex says. "She is a tough old bird," her physician tells me.

"Your mother could have run General Motors!" my Aunt Pat says.

At her nursing home in Lakewood, Colorado, Mom has a sort-of-boyfriend, Ray. When I come to her room and Ray visits, he looks at me and says with a devilish grin, "He needs help with his hearing." Ray is referring to my mother.

This nettles me. "Why do you call my mother a 'he'?"

"He wears men's clothes." Ray points at Mom's denim jacket and Levi jeans. I take a good look at her. She is still beautiful, with good bone structure, lovely green eyes, and white hair. And she has a great figure for jeans. That's why she wears them.

I say to Ray, "Men don't usually wear makeup, earrings, and necklaces—and get their hair done."

"But he's a he."

If my mother is a "he," then what am I?

Before moving into the nursing home, she lives in her own home in Golden. My mother, eighty-six-years-old, calls me one day and says in a soft voice, "Mary, how would you like to go to Antarctica?"

I pause. She seems vulnerable, not the same strong cowgirl woman she used to be. She has mini-strokes and is hard of hearing. But I admire her courage.

"Antarctica, Mom? Are you serious?" I ask. Traveling with her would be challenging, and that's an understatement.

"Yes, I'm serious. I've always wanted to go to Antarctica."

〜〜〜〜〜〜〜〜〜

From Denver International Airport, we fly overnight and finally board the Russian icebreaker in Ushaia, on the southern tip of Argentina. When our ship crosses the Drake Passage, where the Pacific and Atlantic Oceans crash together, the ship rocks hard for twenty-four hours. Many passengers wear patches on their necks for seasickness and Mom stays in bed all day. She announces, "Mary, if I die on this ship, you throw my body overboard. But first take out my gold teeth!"

"You can't die here—I forgot my pliers," I say. But inside I am considering how tough my mother is. Maybe that's the way to be in old age; you have more adventures. But in spite of her boldness, she says, "I'm going to stay on the ship while you go see the penguins."

I bristle. "No way, Mom," I say. "We traveled all the way down here to Antarctica together. The penguins are our reward, a once-in-a-lifetime experience."

"I guess if you risked riding those steers in rodeos, I could risk the Zodiac ride out to see the penguins."

"Way to go, Mom!"

The wind blows hard at forty knots. Wrapped in red parkas, Mom and I ride in the inflatable Zodiac rocking over the whitecaps, with ten other people out to an island. The penguins stand in groups surveying us as we climb onto land. Mom's eyes widen as she studies the appealing penguins. She's a bit wobbly as I hold her arm. "Great courage, Mom. I'm proud of you."

"I will never forget this as long as I live," she says.

Luckily she survives Antarctica, and I don't have to pull out her gold teeth. In Argentina on the way back home, adventures continue. When we dine at an elegant hotel in Buenos Aires, Mom orders filet of sole. She consumes half of it and takes the rest to the room in a doggy bag. The next night we are back in the same restaurant and after the waiter takes my order, Mom plucks the doggy bag out of her purse and says to the waiter, "Heat this up, please."

"No problem, madam," he says politely. I put my napkin over my face and slide halfway under the table. When I tell this story to a fellow traveler later, he says, "Your mother has balls. Brass balls."

When we got home safely to Colorado, Mom said, "That was the greatest trip I ever took. I loved every minute of it."

My mother was one of a kind—a heck of a lot of fun. If she was a "he," then maybe a "he" is the thing to be.

Colorado Community Media newspapers, March 2012

Mom, 86, and me in Antarctica, 2005

41

The Path to Inspired Writing

Over the years scribes have interviewed authors such as Geoffrey Chaucer, William Shakespeare, Voltaire, Mark Twain, Robert Benchley, Erma Bombeck, and Dave Barry. But so far I must have missed the knock on the door.

Now, to be prepared, I've collected the following notes for a journalist about how I write, when one comes to my house.

Supplies

For my first draft I use an 8½ ×11 lined yellow pad, a clipboard, and a gel pen. A gel pen permits your emotions to go directly from your heart, down your arm, and onto the paper.

A cat makes a helpful prop while you are writing. My feline stretches across my lap and puts her paw on my right hand as I write.

When the piece is finished, I lay the yellow pad on the floor for my cat to walk across. His muddy footprints on my writing might explain my transitional jumps and spotty logic.

Inspiration

How do I come up with ideas for stories? How much comes from inspiration and how much from Starbucks Colombian coffee?

I get dressed, drink a pot of coffee, and gaze at my kitchen table covered with detritus of cornflakes, notebooks, and old newspapers—and then go sit in my writing chair.

I'm wearing my writing outfit: a zippered hoodie, slacks, and striped toe socks. After hours and hours of waiting for a topic or a leading sentence, I ask for help from above. Believe me, at some point during the day if I stay in the chair long enough, my eyes begin to sparkle and my pen moves across the page. Words flow.

At first it might be just my name and address, but then I feel a rumble inside and the story begins to rock.

Content

Long ago I realized it would take more brainpower than I possess to write political commentary. More dangerous for me would be to fire off potshots at political leaders. When I took hunter safety, the instructor notified me that I couldn't use the sight on the rifle because I'm left-eye dominant and right-handed.

When I put the rifle butt on my right shoulder and lined up my left eye on the sight, I twisted my body like a pretzel and was cock-eyed. What does that have to do with verbal potshots at politicians, you ask? Just trust me, it does. I've learned from experience that political commentary is not my territory.

In the end, I've discovered through fits and starts it's wiser for me to write about less incendiary topics such as riding a steer in a rodeo, talking turkeys, or conversations with seagulls.

In my case, writing a good piece isn't like quilting or baking, for it must come from deep in my emotions, from some ruckus inside me clamoring to get out.

If you have no surge of feelings within yourself, you can always brew a strong pot of coffee and go sit in your writing chair with your gel pen aimed at your writing pad. If after hours and hours you still don't have inspiration, you can pray for a kick-start from heaven.

This column was inspired by Robert Benchley's "How I Create."
Colorado Community Media newspapers, 2012

Mia, my greatest critic

42

Spring Cleaning Reminds Me of My Mother

The Native Americans say white women have too many possessions that need dusting. They're right. As I'm doing early spring inventory at my house, I am reminded of cleaning out my mother's house years ago.

My mother had moved into a nursing home and because her house was to be sold, as the only daughter I volunteered to act as chief sorter of family items.

For a few minutes I picture myself in Mom's house before it was sold.

As I face the motherless house, decisions, like a flock of barnyard geese, peck and hiss at me.

Trophies wink from the mantle of my mother's kitchen and bring up memories of the good old days when Mom and I competed in gymkhanas and horse shows together. What to do with those trophies?

After notifying my kids about their grandmother's move and that her house would be sold, my son arrives from college. He says, "Mother, please don't sell Grandma's house, where they loved me all my life. You should move in here."

Ouch, I feel a twinge of his pain. I explain to him that I would feel isolated living by myself in Mom's house. He sadly faces the facts and chooses some things of his grandparents to save. My daughter arrives from Chicago. With a good eye, she chooses furniture, paintings, antique jewelry, and fans from her favorite grandmother's place.

After my daughter and son leave, I sit at the kitchen table in the house where I was raised. In my hands I tenderly hold a framed photo of my older brother looking handsome in his U.S. Navy pilot's uniform. Since he is mentally disabled and not available to help me, I have to figure out what to do with his camping equipment, Linda Ronstadt posters, and Beach Boys albums. These items have been stored by my mother for over twenty years in a bomb shelter–style storeroom.

This cement basement cavern behind the furnace room contains fishing equipment, cardboard cartons stuffed with financial papers, war memorabilia, and handwritten love letters written between my parents during World War II.

I'm happy to find these letters, real treasures, and also discover every letter I wrote to my parents when I was in college in New York.

But after a day sorting items into boxes labeled "save," "estate sale," "garage sale," or "trash," I feel drained and overwhelmed.

The Native Americans are right about white women having too many objects. Out of desperation I grimace and invite my ex-husband to go through giant piles of family photos on the ping-pong table in the recreation room. I hope he'll take some of the snapshots of our family off my hands. After he briefly pitches in and snares a few old pictures, he says, "This is staggering."

Then we go upstairs and as he's leaving, he says smoothly, "Could I have your mother's turquoise-covered longhorn skull? And also the model of the B-24 your father was shot down in?"

No, yes, I mean no, not so fast. Help me, God.

Wearing tennis clothes, my mother's best friend, Dorothy, opens the screen door and asks, "Is everything OK, Mary?"

The family accountant, who is a close friend of my mother's, shows up and helps with the numbers. We look at the framed photos of Mom with congressmen and senators on the wall of her office.

With mixed feelings of relief to get the house cleaned out and longing for the past, I wonder what it all means. Does God have a plan? I shove my grief deep down inside, but it is like an ocean wave that rocks forth at high tide.

Eventually I get the job done, with most of my hair intact, and life moves on. I sell Mom's house for a fair price and put the money in her account. She enjoys visiting with the staff at the nursing home, and she loves not having so much stuff to worry about.

Now in my own house, as I get ready for spring cleaning, I go through my inventory. I still have all the letters from Mom's house and haven't read them yet. But along with that I have too much on paper, too many photos, too many cell phone chargers.

Maybe the Native Americans are right. I'm a white woman collecting too much dusty stuff. My husband and I have talked about setting up a tepee in the backyard where we could go meditate on the theory of simplicity.

It might be a good idea before it's too late and my kids are sorting through my things and saying, "Why the heck did she have three backpacks, ten pairs of sunglasses, and fifteen purses? And why did she keep those notebooks full of those columns she wrote?"

"You better not throw those out," I'll warn from the beyond.

Colorado Community Media newspapers, March 2013

Part Six

Out to Pasture? Not a Chance

There is a fountain of youth: it is your mind, your talents, the creativity you bring to your life and the lives of people you love. When you learn to tap this source, you will truly have defeated age.
—Sophia Loren

43

Arte Johnson, "Verrry Interesting"

How did I get invited to an intimate black tie dinner with Arte Johnson—the man who is famous for saying "Verrry interesting" and getting hit over the head with a purse by Ruth Buzzi on the television comedy show *Laugh-In*?

The Benchley group invited me because my essay "The Truth about Steam Baths" made me one of the "top ten funny writers" in the 2012 Robert Benchley National Humor Writing Contest.

As a lifelong fan of Arte Johnson, I wanted to talk with him. In addition, I wanted to get to know the Robert Benchley Society folks who live back East, who I only knew through e-mail. The Robert Benchley Society Annual Award for Humor dinner was held at the exclusive Jonathan Beach Club Penthouse in Santa Monica, California, overlooking the Pacific Ocean. We dined at a big table, which reminded me of the famous Algonquin Round Table group of which Benchley was a member, along with Dorothy Parker.

The only person from the Rocky Mountain states, I felt camaraderie with this group of Bostonians, New Yorkers, and Washington, D.C., people. Was it Robert Benchley's spirit that held us together? I did, however, feel self-conscious about my dress and wondered if it qualified for "black tie." Tim French, a man from Alabama, the 2012 champion, claimed he couldn't give an entertaining acceptance speech. He panicked when the button from his tux popped off and disappeared down a grate. One might wonder if his worrywart style was purposeful, because it was hysterical. Maybe after writing for the contest, some of us took on Benchley's characteristics. His writing, much of it published in *The New Yorker* and *Vanity Fair* beginning in the 1920s, covered universal subjects such as reading the Sunday funnies aloud to the kiddies, or mirrors that seem to take delight in making one's reflection look bad.

⌒

Bright-eyed Arte Johnson, a five-foot-tall pistol, says, "I loved Benchley's humor and admired that it was clean. When I was a kid, I adored Benchley in short comedic films that were shown before feature films. His shape reminded me of an avocado." He adds, "And just so you know, I don't go to these black tie dinners anymore. I had to look in the crawl space for my bow tie!" At eighty-three, white-haired Arte's every word keeps us riveted.

⌒

Later the Benchley attendees meet at a Venice art studio. I read out loud a Benchley-inspired piece I wrote called "How to Do Nothing for a Day." To my delight, they laugh at the jokes about writers falling asleep at conferences.

I hope to win first in the Benchley contest someday.

And if I attend the yearly gathering, so I don't wobble in high heels, I'll wear a vintage dress with my red cowboy boots.

Colorado Community Media newspapers, 2012

44

The Truth About Steam Baths

Smoke signals from the east tell of a Robert Benchley writing contest—but can a female scribbler compose a piece in the master's style?

While drinking a martini, I read Benchley's essay "Sporting Life in America: Turkish Bathing." To do research on this topic, I plot a trip to the local steam baths on Ladies Day.

But first I must have one more martini. Although the place is located in a historic neighborhood, rumor has it no one has been shot with an arrow.

At the desk, I receive a tiny towel.

What to cover with it? I suppose I could wear it like loincloth.

In the locker room, I covet a hula skirt with an elastic waistband. A sympathetic woman whispers, "Nobody's perfect."

Phew.

I butt into the main steam room, where women with relaxed eyes soak in hot pools. I wonder if they have been chewing leaves because they remind me of the Lotus Eaters Island People from the Greek epic *The Odyssey*. Will I become so limp I never leave and they have to carry me out on a stretcher?

The corner hot tub entices me and I descend into the cauldron. A fellow bather promises, "You'll get used to it," but I don't. After five minutes of boiling myself, I wobble out like an inebriated cockatoo.

A stocky matron holds a bristle-covered brick and asks me, "Do you want a scrub?"

"Not now, but if I pass out, have your way with me."

A slippery chair becomes my seat, but it's too damp to text or knit. Perhaps I could try meditating, but my mantra evades me. All that comes to mind is "Shugga bugga."

While exploring in the back, I discover the hotter steam room, which looks like a monster's cave. After prying open the door, the steam blasts me. The outline of a bench appears and I perch on my terry cloth square. Each breath feels like I'm inhaling scouring pads. Like a true masochist, I savor the torture and am sure it is doing me some good. All four of my cheeks burn.

At some point later, a glimpse in the mirror reveals my face, which appears to have one eye and no hair. Have I turned into the Cyclops? I glance away and spot a star athlete from my high school class. Gasp, where can I hide? But we are face to face.

"What a surprise to see you here," I say, not admitting I have forgotten her name.

"Yes, yes." She's also forgotten mine.

"How's your tennis?"

"I won a match in Wimbledon."

"Congratulations."

"Thanks. And what are you up to?"

"Have you heard of Robert Benchley?"

"I thought you were Robert Benchley."

I chuckle. "And I thought you were Richard Simmons."

"Ha!" She swats me with an imaginary tennis racket.

My masseuse rescues me. The tennis player and I say our fond good-byes. After a dainty massage, I call the masseuse a wimp and she calls me a taxi.

Robert Benchley?

Is he in heaven having a good time with his cronies, laughing? I hope so.

The taxi drops me off at my favorite bar and after a stiff drink I talk my writer friends into toasting the master.

This essay was a semifinalist in the
2012 Robert Benchley National Humor Writing Contest.

45

Talking Hair

Some lucky people have such thick, smooth, and shiny hair that you can't take your eyes off it. These people are blessed with "good hair." They are chosen as homecoming queens and kings, win beauty contests, and may be elected to be president of the United States. I envy these people because I have bad hair.

When I have a special event to attend, my own "naughty hair" plays tug-of-war with me and runs me around the block. And it loves to talk. The conversation goes like this:

Hair says, "Stop trying to smooth me out!"

"But I need you to look gorgeous," I say.

"Forget it. I'm in a limp and snaky mood."

"Yikes, I hate snakes."

"Think Medusa."

"No way," I say. "I'm going to my high school reunion."

"Blecch. I can't stand those dweebs."

"Now, settle down."

"Dream on."

I picture my old friends from my high school class with tidy hair who will be at the reunion. "Please, hair. I'll make it worth your while. I'll use your favorite chocolate mint conditioner."

"Hmmm. I'll think about it."

After shampooing and styling my locks I look in the mirror and shudder. My hair looks like a tumbleweed. I pick up the hairspray.

"I want to flip up," Hair says.

"You look like a bush. Mama says it's time to lie down and smile."

"Ha, ha, ha."

"Just this once could you cooperate? I'm going to be photographed and put on Facebook."

"How boring."

"And YouTube."

"Good, I want to act up on the Internet."

"You're in a contrary mood, Hair."

"I'm in a great mood. I've never felt friskier."

I wonder if I have bad karma. Or just bad k'hairma. I look in the mirror and know it's hopeless. No wonder beauticians charge me so much—they have to work miracles. Regretting that I didn't line up a styling appointment, I remind myself to plan better next time. When my hair looks like a bush, it makes my face look like a pancake. I ferret out my favorite sequined cowboy hat.

"Not that hat," Hair says. "It will cover me. I want to be noticed. I want to be the star of the show."

"I'm wearing shorts and cowboy boots," I say. "My classmates will check out my great legs and red cowboy boots instead of you."

"Aaaaghhh! You're killing me."

"Enough!"

"You look like a barrel racer."

Thoughts of my horse and rodeo days make me happy. I adjust my hat and smile.

"But I wanted you to wear a dress," Hair says. "I'm going to have a nervous breakdown."

Hair having a nervous breakdown? I thought I was the one panicking. With an epiphany, I realize that my hair has immature qualities, right to the core. But possibly, just maybe immaturity isn't all negative.

In the past, I used to feel sorry for myself and complain because I had "bad hair." But I've had a change in my attitude. I've come to treasure the way my hair chatters and spouts off. Who wants to be queen of the ball or president anyway? I'd rather have wild adventures with my companion, my naughty hair.

Colorado Community Media newspapers, April 2012

46

Out of Candy Panic

When I was a kid, I looked forward to Halloween. As costumed children approached our door, they heard my father's deep voice over a loud speaker: "Don't step on the dead body."

One little girl said, "I won't."

It was fun as a child, but now that I'm an adult, Halloween makes me edgy. The darkness, the spooks, and the zombies give me the creeps.

My husband and I moved into a new house last summer and we didn't know what to expect on October 31. "I'll bet we don't get too many trick-or-treaters," I said. "People take their kids to shopping malls these days."

As soon darkness falls, the doorbell sounds, "Ding dong." A little ghost, monster, and goblin converge at the door. They chirp, "Trick or treat." We hand out Snickers Bars, Milky Ways, and Butterfingers and wish them well. But with a steady stream of costumed kids for an hour, we're almost out of treats.

"I'll go to the market," my hubby volunteers, anxious to get away. Holy Toledo. I'll be alone at the house on Halloween—with no candy. Would the kids play tricks? Put eyeballs on our lawn? Turn gophers loose in the garden? Bring bats onto the porch?

When I pass out the last Milky Way, I make a circle of cushions on the lawn and light a candle. Voices in the street sound like ghouls. Marmaduke, a tiny Lady Gaga, Barack Obama, a ghost, and a tall zombie approach me. "Trick or treat!"

"Jokes are your treat," I say. "Have a seat."

They form a circle. "Who was the most famous skeleton detective?" I ask.

"We don't know, who?"

"Sherlock Bones."

They groan.

"Don't you kids have a sense of humor?" I counter.

"We want candy, lots and lots of candy," they counter back.

"OK, here's another one. Where do baby goblins go during the day?"

"We give up," they howl.

"Dayscare centers."

Marmaduke growls from deep down inside. I hadn't expected such a tough audience.

"Trick or treat!" they shout. I stare at the ghost. "What do you call a ghost who gets too close to the bonfire?"

"What?"

"A ghost toasty."

Lady Gaga giggles. A glimmer of hope. Jokes might work instead of candy. But my mind freezes up like a shopping cart that reaches the boundary of a parking lot.

"We want candy, we want candy," they chant. A gang of moaning vampires trots toward me from the street. I clutch my throat. I'm sure I feel blood.

My husband screeches into the driveway with bags of caramels and chocolates. We rip open the bags, shell out candy to the kids. To calm my frazzled nerves I stuff a Snickers Bar into my mouth. Delicious. The sugar and caffeine hype me up.

"That was close," I gasp to my monster, I mean my husband.

Next Halloween we'll prepare better. We'll fill the car with Hershey bars, Jolly Ranchers, M&M's and Reese's Peanut Butter Cups.

And I'm telling better jokes.

Colorado Community Media newspapers, October 2011

47

Talking Turkey

Thanksgiving is a day when men tear their hair out watching football games on television while women stress out over preparing turkeys.

Last year I hosted a Thanksgiving feast for family and friends. The challenge was the bird.

Three days before Thanksgiving I had a dream: In the dream I chased Herbert, my turkey, around the backyard with a butcher knife. I wore a gun in my holster in case things got ugly.

He let out a mind-warping shriek and bolted through the bushes into the neighbor's yard.

Mrs. Nostrum, my neighbor, spotted me. "What are you doing with that knife, Mary?"

"It's obvious. Herbert has had a good run and now it's time for him to fulfill his greater destiny," I said. "Why don't you hold his head for me?"

Racing toward Mrs. Nostrum, Herbert flapped his wings and cried, "Rescue me!"

Scooping up the turkey in her arms, she said, "There, there, Herbert, come to Mama. I'll take care of you."

Herbert cooed and laid his head on her shoulder. Watching her holding Herbert, I realized even though he was a game bird, I was fond of the fluffy creature. But I also knew he would make a spectacular dinner. I mustered up all the authority I could and said, "Mrs. Nostrum, I need Herbert. Give me my turkey back."

"No! Please, no," Herbert moaned. His tears soaked Mrs. Nostrum's blouse.

She stroked his head. "Don't you worry, Herbert, you're safe now with me."

She carried Herbert into her house. "Hey, you thief, come back here!" I said.

Standing on Mrs. Nostrum's front porch, I spotted Herbert through the window. My turkey and I had eye contact. He squawked and scurried under the dining room table. My neighbor's toddler son scrambled up next to Herbert and hugged him.

Aw shucks, I felt mushy.

My eyes flew open and the turkey dream ended abruptly. Phew!

From my bedside table I picked up a magazine with a photo of a perfect Thanksgiving turkey dinner with mashed potatoes, gravy, and pumpkin pie. I could almost taste the succulent pumpkin pie. I had left my shopping to the last minute and wondered if that's what caused the nightmare. I had to get my food act together before I'd sleep another wink.

In my bathrobe and slippers, I drove to the supermarket and surveyed a bin full of frozen turkeys, white and hermetically sealed. They resembled frozen balls, ammo for an arctic cannon.

I reluctantly selected a cannonball labeled "Turkey."

In my heart of hearts, I prayed the turkey never, ever had been named Herbert.

Colorado Community Media newspapers, November 2011

48

Bachelor's Degree in Hobo Studies

"Aren't you worried your son will be squished hopping freight trains?" my friend asks me.

"Sure, sometimes. But he's good at it. He's been doing it since he was a junior at Colorado State University," I say. "That's where he got started hitching rides on the trains as they run through Fort Collins. CSU awarded him a degree in hobo studies."

"What does he eat?"

"Whatever he can find," I say. "He talks about finding food in dumpsters, especially Kentucky Fried Chicken."

My friend laughs. "Does he go for the original?"

"Actually, he likes the crispy. It probably reminds him of my cooking—charred thighs and drumsticks, charred everything."

Over Memorial Day this year, I fly up to visit him in Seattle where he is stationed with the Coast Guard.

He treats me to dinner at a French restaurant in the quaint seaside town of Edmunds, Washington. Freight trains run by a stone's throw from the eating establishment. Clackety-clack, clackety-clack.

With the hearing of a fox, Jim knows when a train is approaching from miles away. He slips over to the window to watch.

After dinner we cross the tracks on foot and walk along the sliver of beach for a hundred feet or so. He spots a light in the distance, which looks like a house light to me. "One's coming," he says. We wait and wait but no train. We head for the crossing, the spot where we had crossed earlier, that leads back into town.

Suddenly the southbound freight train he had spotted comes meandering and clanking through, with tanks of magnesium chloride, stacks of Weyerhauser lumber wrapped in white paper, and tanks of unknown liquids wrapped in who knows what. The train's presence exhilarates me—the smell of oil and grease is the train's calling card.

With just a subtle puff of air from the train, Jim says, "It broke air, which means the brakes have gone out."

The mile-long freight train screeches to a halt, blocking the crossing. The train's cars stretch a mile in either direction down the tracks.

"This train won't be moving for two hours," Jim says.

I start to feel giddy and nervous being trapped on the wrong side of the tracks with Jim's car out of our reach. We stare at the boxcars and extra high lumber cars.

Calmly, like a professional, Jim figures out how to get us across. A couple near us discusses the same topic. My eyes scan under the wheels. "I'm not crawling under there!" I declare.

"No problem. It's easy," Jim says, indicating a boxcar. Just climb up this rung and onto this ledge. Don't worry, Mom, this train isn't going to move."

Goosebumps cover my arms as I consider the risk. I grit my teeth and step up on the rung and pull myself up. The train vibrates but doesn't move. I tiptoe sideways across this narrow six-inch ledge. Nervously, I put my foot down on the one rung on the other side. Jim helps me down. Ground never felt so good! We're on the right side of the tracks.

People start following our example. Jim becomes the train's spokesman to confused people stopped in cars and on foot. He explains, "The brakes are out and it will be a while." He doesn't tell anyone what to do, but many trapped on the wrong side of the tracks continue to take the matter into their own hands.

As more people climb across the boxcar, a train official wearing orange shouts, "Get off the train!" We move back, but Jim still won't leave the area near the train. Why? Because he loves the big old hunk of traveling machinery. We wait until it leaves.

What a night. It was the closest to riding a freight train I've ever experienced. A freight train's presence wakes up every cell in your body as if it's a dangerous wild animal to be respected.

When I return home to Colorado from Washington, my friend says, "He's twenty-eight now. Don't you think you should get your son to stop hopping trains?"

I smile. "I've tried but it's no use. Can you stop the wind?"

Colorado Community Media newspapers, June 2013

49

I'm Jealous of a Black Bear

I'm jealous of a black bear in Estes Park. It's December and workers discovered him hibernating in a crawl space under their business. So while workers sweat, strain, and bear down on their work in the office, the bear gets to sleep—right under their feet. They can hear him shifting around at times and hope he won't pop his head up through the floor and say, "Here's Johnny."

I'm jealous because the bear has no holiday stress, no gift shopping, or New Year's resolutions. He sticks his tongue out at social pressure.

He is the master of the forest.

After Christmas I am exhausted and want to sleep for days to catch up from lost rest. If I could hibernate, I could wake up refreshed, ready for the New Year along about March. Who needs January and February anyway?

Yes, this bear is tucked away in a cozy space with the comforting rhythm of computers clicking. He may wake up and demand, "I'm occupying this place until you give me an iPad."

According to an article in the *Estes Park News* by Kris Hazelton, the Colorado Division of Wildlife gives advice for evicting the bear: "Put ammonia rags down in the crawl space and play loud rock music." The office workers try this technique, but the bear doesn't budge.

(This reminds me of when I was blasted with Def Leppard heavy metal CDs and smelly socks belonging to my teenage son. I should have hibernated like the bear under the office.)

During bear hibernation, which begins in November or December, the bruin's heart slows from forty to fifty beats per minute to eight beats per minute.

If the office black bear is a pregnant female, the office staff will hear noise from the cubs in February. That part of bearhood I would not be excited about—waking up with crying babies.

My daughter says, "I'd like hibernation pregnancy, so I'd sleep through all the discomfort."

Native Americans honor bears as sacred animals and believe during hibernation bears leave behind their big hairy bodies and travel to the spirit world, where they revitalize and obtain healing powers.

If I hibernated, I would probably come back so refreshed no one would recognize me. I could hang out a sign on my office door: "Mary's Healing Powers."

The black bear reminds the office workers daily to slow down. The spirit world of peace enters the human world of business.

While staying at YMCA of the Rockies in Estes Park with my family after Christmas, I take a rest.

Imagining I'm a black bruin sleeping under an office, I am no longer jealous. Before too long the bear becomes my spirit animal. I purchase a small diamond bear necklace, clasp it around my neck, and never take it off.

Colorado Community Media newspapers, January 2012

50

How to Do Nothing

I am a woman who knows how to do nothing, and I suspect I am getting a reputation for this skill. In the morning I wake up and walk outside. Dandelions sprout and go to seed on my front lawn and I say, "Hello, dandelions, hello bindweed, good morning!"

My motto is: Never pull a weed today that will grow more colorful and glorious tomorrow.

Cooking? It's been too hot to cook. Sure, in the morning I have ambitions for a few seconds, but by noon the air conditioner has quit and a few relatives have showed up. We sit around the living room and stare at each other at mealtime. My eye gleams. If I don't walk in the kitchen, someone will finally volunteer to cook or suggest a restaurant.

If I fear hunger will ruin my resolve, I say, "I must lie down since I've had a long day." I remember the stash of snacks in the bedroom, and I disappear, close the door of the boudoir, and scarf down a can of sardines.

In the summer friends ask me, "Mary, what are you up to lately?"

I say, "Oh, I'm working on my novel." Ha! Writing fiction is the greatest cover known to man or woman for doing nothing. I figured out long ago, after years of kidding myself, that writing one page a day of my novel was getting me nowhere, except to fool other people into thinking I am a writer.

Don't tell anyone, but the notes and scribbles for my novel still lie in a box under my bed. I move the box around every day, sometimes just jot down a few lines.

A neighbor asks how my novel is going.

"I'm working on the characterization," I say. "This takes much contemplation."

Another day I might explain to someone who asks about my novel, "I'm working on the theme."

An attractive place to do nothing is writers' conferences. Wearing dark glasses, I stare intently at the speaker until my eyes begin to close. Sometimes I bring a neck brace so my chin won't nod forward. "Oh yes, I have whiplash," I tell anyone who asks.

That is, if I'm awake.

If the speaker is talking about writing a memoir, I quietly chuckle. I know that for my memoir, I can just dig out a few photos, paste them on a page, and scrawl notes next to them. Then I can claim I'm working on my memoir, but since I can't remember what happened forty years ago, it creates a challenge. So each day when I'm pretending to write my memoir, I either take a nap or go outside and talk to the weeds.

You see, this "do nothing lifestyle" isn't for everyone, but it definitely agrees with me.

Colorado Community Media newspapers, August 2012

51

Usual Suspect on the Airport Train

*No one can understand the truth until he drinks
of coffee's frothy goodness.*
—Shik Abdal Kadir

I f you think I'm kidding about this you're wrong. Over Memorial
Day I went to visit my son, Jim, in Seattle who was stationed on
the *Polar Sea*, a U.S. Coast Guard icebreaker. Due to mischievous
mechanical goblins, the ship has dropped anchor permanently. And
due to so much time in port, Jim rented an apartment in which I
stayed for three days. My offspring stocked up with everything but
coffee. No problem. A Seattle coffee shop next door kept me supplied
with my morning cup Sunday and Monday.

But on my departure day, Tuesday morning Jim has to be at the
Coast Guard station at 6:45 a.m. The airport lies an hour away and
my plane is due to leave at 8:55 a.m. I volunteer to take the light rail
to the Seattle-Tacoma airport. Way past cool. What an adventure. But
a giant crisis begins to build—the coffee shop next door isn't open in
time for me to get my daily dose of caffeine.

Jim drops me off at the light rail station and gives me $2 for the
train fare. Oh, this will be easy, I think, never having taken Seattle's
train before. A person will sell me a ticket and then I'll step through

a turnstile, like on the subway years ago in New York City. (True confession: I along with other college students sneaked under the turnstile in NYC and didn't pay.)

But now I'm way past college and I don't snappily negotiate new ticket systems. Carrying my suitcase I descend the stairs and discover I'm on the wrong side of the tracks. I climb up and then downstairs to the other side. Still foggy from lack of caffeine, I board the train.

"So how do you pay on this thing?" I ask the woman behind me.

"You buy the ticket before you get on," she says. We rumble along the tracks past trees and houses. Just then, two stocky creatures in black uniforms with guns in holsters approach me. One has a jacket that says "Security" and the other "Fare Police." I wish I had a walker, a cane, or an oxygen tank so they could see I'm handicapped. But caffeine deprivation doesn't have a visual symbol.

"Where's your ticket?" the woman barks.

"Here's my $2." I hand the bills to her.

"We can't take your money. Give us your ID."

I fish out my passport. Still frosty the Fare Police woman photographs it and asks for my current address. She types it in her handheld computer. I feel confused, bewildered, and anxious as to what they will do with me. Take me to jail?

She stares at my passport. "I've never been to Seattle or ridden light rail before," I say, trying to gain her sympathy. But her eyes are cold as those of a guard dog. Her expression says, "I've seen your type before."

Maybe she has seen my type. Maybe her mother and father worked in the New York subways and remember me from when I crawled under the subway turnstiles. They probably told her about me. I feel shaky and guilty, my thoughts scrambling through my mind.

"Normally there's a $150 fine," the Fare Police woman says. "Just this one time we'll let you go. You have a record now and we'll get you if you ever do this again. We'll get you."

"OK, OK. I won't do it again," I promise. And believe me I mean it. But in spite of my stress and embarrassment, I do get a free ride to the Seattle-Tacoma airport! I feel energized, which makes me wonder if I have the heart of a thief relishing the theft.

And at the airport, after security, I stop at a Seattle's Best coffee shop. This usual suspect on the airport train savors the frothy goodness of a mug of Colombian coffee.

Ah, the day should go better now.

Colorado Community Media newspapers, June 2011

52

Ten Ways to Become a Scatterbrain

Listen up, this is important. When I was in fourth grade at Maple Grove Elementary School eons ago, I aced a magazine test. It was titled, "Are You a Scatterbrain?" (*Webster's Dictionary* says a scatterbrain is anybody incapable of concentration or serious thought.) I scored higher than any other student in my class.

Since my elementary school days, it has become easier for ordinary people to become a scatterbrain—due to changes in technology. Tricky marketers with no surplus of conscience have taken over every area of our lives and sold us on the idea that more is better, newer is better, and faster is better. The more stuff we buy, the harder it is to focus and make good decisions, and they know it.

I don't know about you, but my brain cannot keep up with the pace of change in technology. My daily choices multiply like rabbits. Although I had a period of relief during my late forties after the kids left the house and I could concentrate for a few minutes, it was short-lived.

"Oh, she's just a scatterbrain," people say. At least it gives me an identity. Less judgmental types relate to this part of me because they are also scatterbrains and don't feel so alone.

If you've been hiding out in the woods, focused but bored to death, here's my advice of how to become a top-of-the-line scatterbrain:

1. Get an iPhone. Send texts to your family and friends every hour. Talk on the phone as much as possible so your body will be in one place and your brain will be in another place.

2. At 7 a.m. look out the window and get dressed for the way the weather appears. At noon you will either be freezing because you underdressed or overheated because you overdressed. Your mind will flicker with the rapid changes in weather as you switch from heat to air conditioning and back to heat in your vehicle.

3. Go to a deli restaurant and choose between forty-five sandwiches with choices of bread suggested by the counterperson: "white, wheat, rye, non-gluten, panini, toasted or untoasted, buttered or unbuttered." If you're having a side dish, you will be asked, "Baked potato, mashed, fries, quinoa, or rice, cold slaw or green beans? Noodles made of wheat or rice?" Scatter your brain around that!

4. Watch every murder trial and crime show on TV, and let your mind dwell on the details while you are paying your bills.

5. Watch *Jeopardy*. Flunk all the answers to questions like, What Roman emperor invaded Ireland in the first century B.C.? Fill your mind with the worthless trivia you learn each night and watch the contestants make big bucks.

6. Every time the cat meows, feed her.

7. Accept five invitations in a week where you are required to bring "a dish."

8. Check your e-mail every hour and save everything due to indecision until you have a long kite tail of at least a thousand messages.

9. When online, click on every popup.

10. Switch from your old computer software to a new, more complicated word processing system. When four-letter words don't fix it, throw your computer in the lake.

If you live in the heart of the American culture, you may already be doing all the things on my list. If not, give it a try. You may succeed in becoming a scatterbrain.

Colorado Community Media newspapers, April 2014

53

Alligator Bites Grandma's Umbrella

I hunker down under my umbrella on the wood walkway at Gatorland, a live alligator park just south of Orlando, Florida. It rains so hard, snakes and baby alligators appear with the deluge. I have come with my grandkids during late December.

A gust of wind suddenly rips my umbrella out of my hands and dumps it into the swamp water. An enormous green alligator with bubble eyes that look human, and a nose as long as my legs, glides forward. He closes his jaws on my red, yellow, and blue polka-dot umbrella. In shock, my mouth drops open. He appears to be chowing down on my umbrella! Maybe he thinks there's a person attached to it.

The rain drenches my hair and droplets run down my blouse.

A Gatorland worker using a long pole with a loop at the end fishes down in the murky water attempting to lasso my umbrella. The alligator snaps at the loop. As the worker kneels on the railing, I gasp. "Sir, please don't risk your life for my umbrella," I say. "It can be replaced. I bought it at Target."

A second worker appears and holds the first worker's belt loops as he crawls forward onto the flimsy rope net attached to the railing. I fear I'm about to see an alligator swallow a man.

Eight times the worker plunges his pole deep into the murky water with no results. I'm sure it's a goner.

Ye of little faith. Out of the depths of darkness, the worker plucks my umbrella, open with the fabric still intact. The spring and handle appear to be working.

"Unbelievable!" I say. "You are amazing. Thank you so much!"

After shaking the water off my umbrella, I put it back into use, holding it over my head. Now protected from the rain by an umbrella that had been in an alligator's mouth, I feel swampy as trickles run down my back.

The thick smell of humidity, which has turned my hair into a giant mass of curls, now fogs up my glasses. I tell my grandson, "Grandma just had an exciting encounter with an alligator."

"Yay, Grandma!" he says.

Later, at the Wild Side BBQ restaurant, my daughter orders deep-fried alligator bites, which taste delicious—morsels dipped in "Special Sauce." Maybe they mix the sauce with swamp water, but it sure does hit the spot. We order a second plate.

I suddenly remember the big alligator that went after my umbrella. Did he anticipate my dinner when he tried to eat my umbrella for lunch? I'll never know.

Colorado Community newspapers, 2014

Grandma's Gatorland foes, 2013

54

Bike Accident Wake-Up Call

Would someone who is mature please share with me the secret to aging gracefully? I'm at an age high enough in years to qualify for Medicare, but not too old to stay off my bike.

~

After thirty years of riding bikes, and a few harmless falls, I finally do the big one—in the dark. Seeing headlights coming toward me, I hit the brakes hard, way too hard. The bike stops but I don't. I fly over the handlebars and smash my shoulder into the pavement. Pain, ouch, hurt, ache, and more pain.

Unable to move without excruciating pain, I am extracted from the ground to a gurney by ambulance attendants and rushed to the local hospital ER.

After an X-ray, the ER doc announces, "You have a broken humerus—the bone in your right upper arm near your rotator cuff."

"Darn!"

"For the position of the break, we can't set it. You'll wear a sling."

What shocks me for weeks after is how little I can move my arm from my shoulder. I am right-handed, but I have to write and eat with my left hand. My husband has to tie my shoes, which is humbling for me. For six weeks I resemble a war victim wearing a sling. Friendly people who observe my sling tell me myriad tales of other bike accidents resulting in broken collar bones, broken hips, intensive care units, and deaths.

I wonder if someone up above is warning me to stay off my bike? Forever?

After my accident, when I know the damage is limited to my shoulder, I murmur, "Thank God I'm alive—it could have been so much worse."

Time has gone by and I'm out of the sling and the heavy pain, but I'm still in physical therapy for range-of-motion exercises. And I wonder if I want to risk injury again if I get back on the bike?

I'm not sure. Mobility is important to me. In the gym today I ride a bike with a video screen of mountain scenery and it is pleasant and SAFE. Interestingly enough, it is more social than riding outside—I see my friend's mother, Dorothy Haberl, who lives in my old neighborhood. She's almost ninety and still exercising in the gym, an example of aging gracefully.

If aging changes our judgment, as I think it may be doing with mine, how do I gauge what is safe to do? If I don't risk at all, my world will shut down.

I ponder these issues—my own mother stopped exercising after seventy and ended up in a walker in assisted living. Dorothy, my friend's mother, is still out there playing tennis and in her own home.

Unless you believe in reincarnation, the aging process is something we only go through once.

I hope to make wise choices about my activities in the future, and at the same time make the most of my life.

Isn't that what we all want?

Colorado Community Media newspapers, October 10, 2013

55

Interrupting a Writer Is Risky

I'm serious about this: Talk to me as much as you like, I'd love to visit with you, but please don't talk to me before 7 a.m.

You may have seen a movie years back, the classic comedy *As Good as It Gets*. Jack Nicholson plays an eccentric writer living in an apartment across the hall from Greg Kinnear. As Nicholson works on a piece at his word processor, he reads his thoughts out loud to himself: "Love is, love is ..."

A knock is heard on the door. With a look of fury Nicholson flings open his front door, and he lectures Kinnear, his neighbor, "I'm a writer, I work at home all day here. Don't ever, ever knock on this door. Not even if there's a fire, or you hear a thud inside my apartment and a week later smell something, don't knock!"

While watching the movie, I am taken aback by Nicholson's meanness, but the part of me that's a writer understands Nicholson's struggle when he's interrupted in the middle of working on a piece. Because I write early I wish no one would talk to me before 7 a.m. If you stay in our cabin and you hear a rattling in the kitchen before 7 a.m., just pretend a bear has broken into the cabin. You can take discreet photos of the "bear" if you're sneaky about it.

I don't want to be distracted from the deep thought I wake up with by another person's dialogue. Grrr.

"The stove is burning up!" you say.

"Don't panic. Get some water," I say.

"The toilet is overflowing."

"We have an outhouse in the back."

The thought I'm thinking, and quickly losing, may have come out of a dream.

It could involve a vision of how to save the world. If I can stay on track, I will funnel my thought into a column that will light up the newspaper with my glowing brilliance.

"Ha, ha," you say. "I've never read anything brilliant by you, Mary."

Neither have I, but there is always the hope that my insights will help others. If I get spoken to while I'm writing—even "Good morning. How did you sleep?"—my thought will dissipate and I'll get a funny look on my face and the whole day will be set off at an unwelcome angle.

I'll ask myself, What was that creative thought anyway? Did I have a revelation from God?

No. Rather my so-called deep thought was an observation that men and women have different internal thermostats, which causes conflicts on how much the window can be open to let the cool air in.

I wander out the door of the weekend cabin to feel the crisp morning air on my cheeks and see the snow still twinkling in the grass. I feel blessed to be in the Rocky Mountains, even if I've forgotten my creative thought, which wasn't very deep, possibly as shallow as the puddle formed by the melting snow.

And then I have this thought: Maybe it's time to lighten up.

Colorado Community Media newspapers, February 2012

56

Slow Down and Savor

When I was sorting through my mother's old papers after she moved into assisted living, I discovered a page from the *San Francisco Chronicle* dated 1951. The page included a black-and-white photo of a young couple taking a walk together in a field of wild grasses. The man and the woman had peaceful expressions on their faces and were holding hands. It appeared they were blissfully enjoying the day together.

It intrigued me that my mother saved this article titled "Slow Down" by Willard Pleuthner for almost sixty years. Why would my mother, who later in her life became one of the busiest people ever— the woman who my aunt said "could have run General Motors"— maintain space in her desk for a newspaper clipping titled "Slow Down"? I'd love to ask her but it's too late; she's now gone from this world.

The piece "Slow Down" begins:

> Slow me down, Lawd, I's a-goin' too fast,
> I can't see my brother when he's walkin' past.
> I miss a lot o'good things day by day,
> I don't know a blessin' when it comes my way.
> —Old Spiritual

Surprisingly, Pleuthner's 1951 article feels like it was written for me today. Sometimes I rush through life and I don't know why.

My husband, Dick, and I are retired and yet we are both so busy with writing, exercise, volunteer work, and home maintenance that sometimes we lose touch with each other during the day. When I become aware I'm hurrying, I pause, take a deep breath, and try to remember each moment is precious.

Dick and I at times discuss slowing down. But we are constantly tempted to speed up; the push for speed is everywhere: high-speed freeways, high-speed Internet, same-day shipping, instant movies on Netflix, iPhones with e-mail, express lanes, bullet trains. On television and computers we watch events as they happen all over the world and we witness speed records broken in the Olympics by new super-athletes. Television commercials tell us "faster is better."

Adults may adjust to a sped-up life, but how does all this speed affect our children? Pleuthner wrote: "Slow up our weekends of gaiety so we live more with our children … do more with them … grow closer to them. For they need parental companionship now during these uncertain times more than ever before."

My son-in-law and daughter call on the phone and invite me to make a weekly date with my three-year-old grandson, Noah. My eyes sparkle and I adjust my schedule for this important get-together. Noah and I walk in the rain, go to a playground with wet sand, and encounter a slippery earthworm. My grandson looks with wonder at the creature and will probably never forget how it felt tickling the palm of his hand. At the base of the playground slide we create sand animals.

Back home in his room, Noah teaches me how to line up small cars like they're ready for a race. I help him make LEGO garages for the police car and the bad-guy car.

"Grandma Mary, Grandma Mary…" he says later. "Read me *Mike Mulligan and His Steam Shovel.*" He loves stories, and we take each page slowly and talk about the pictures. "Goldilocks and the Three Bears" becomes a favorite.

I'm making an effort to slow down and be present with Noah, and when I'm present with him I feel delighted. Because the gift of presence, like prayer, is intangible, not seen; it is sometimes overlooked as not having value in our hurried-up competitive society.

And now that I'm savoring more time with my husband, and my grandson is becoming a regular part of my life, I'm learning how to "know a blessin' when it comes my way."

Colorado Community Media newspapers, November 2012

A treasure from Mom's clipping collection,
from the *San Francisco Chronicle*, 1950

Acknowledgments

So many people helped me turn my book dreams into a reality. Thank you, from my heart, to all.

Thank you to my English teachers from Wheat Ridge High School, and Buck Hart from the Orme School. Also thanks to the English departments at University of Colorado and Bard College.

Newspaper editors Mikkel Kelly, Glenn Wallace, Mark Ohrenschall, Gil Spencer, and Vincent Carroll have been instrumental professional support.

Jana Clark, Judy Armstrong, Ruth Segal, Maida Blythe, Diane Talon, and Susan Fisher, members of my critique group, provided encouragement along with their helpful comments. Janet Garvey, Colette Smith, Claudia McIntosh, Mary Ozanic, and Kate Barham kindly provided early readings of my manuscript.

Editor Allison St. Claire helped me kick-start this project. After I rode it alone for a while, Jody Rein galloped alongside me and herded the book into the corral.

Father Chris Renner, Rev. Frank Gold, and The Alano Club provided spiritual support just when I needed it most. Shirley Riggs, Sally Faust, Dennis O'Shea, Robbie Knight, and the Robert Benchley Society provided additional inspiration.

My unending gratitude goes to my wonderful family. It is impossible to express enough appreciation to my husband, Dick, my anchor and mainstay who kept my computer running and supported me in immeasurable ways. Also much gratitude to my daughter, Lily, her husband, Wagner, and my son, Jim, all of whom readily provided their love and support throughout this project. And appreciations go to Lily's father-in-law Wagner Sr. and mother-in-law, Shirley, for their kindness and generosity.

Last but not least, a heart full of gratitude goes to my adventurous and loving Mom and Dad. They brought me up with horses and encouraged me as a writer. I still miss them both dearly.

Made in the USA
San Bernardino, CA
26 October 2014